B E S T S E L L I N G   A U T H O R

TERENCE MUNSEY

OBSESSION

MUNSEY MUSIC
Toronto Los Angeles London

This book is entirely a work of fiction. Any resemblance to actual people, places, events, names, incidences, living or dead, is totally coincidental. This work is entirely the product of the author's imagination.

OBSESSION

published by:

MUNSEY MUSIC

Box 511, Richmond Hill, Ontario, Canada, L4C 4Y8

Fax: 905 737 0208

E-Mail: terence_munsey@tvo.org

VISIT OUR WEB SITE@ http://www.digiserve.com/stoneman/

Canadian Cataloguing in Publication Data

Munsey, Terence, 1953-

Obsession

ISBN 0-9697066-5-0

I. Title.

PS8576.U5753027 1997   C813'.54   C97-930114-9

PR9199.3.M86027 1997

Library of Congress Catalogue Number 97–92895

First MUNSEY MUSIC original soft cover printing April 1997

Cover design, and photograph © 1997 by TERENCE MUNSEY

Back cover photo taken by Tracy Goulding

Manufactured in Canada

Acknowledgments

There are many people I wish to thank for all their time, effort, support and encouragement.

Thank you to **Christina Beaumont**, for all her comments and suggestions in the many stages of the manuscript. You have been invaluable to me.
Thank you to Pauline, and then Tracy who read the final manuscript and gave helpful comments.
Thank you to: Lorne, Sandy, Roger, Ron, Karen, Robert Schemmer M.D., and Paula Montana for all their enthusiasm, kindness and friendship.

A very special thank you to the complete **Chapters** organization and all the members of their stores including both **Coles** and **Smithbooks** for their continual outstanding support and commitment to not only my books, but to Canadian authors generally. In particular, I would like to acknowledge and thank **Judith Chant** without whom I would not have a career as a writer today. I will always be indebted to you.

Author's Note

After spending many months on the road doing book signings and promotions for my STONEMAN SERIES™, I began to realize that there were a number of people who were looking for a gripping read within the Mystery—Intrigue—Romance genres. When I met such readers they asked me: 'When was I going to write one?'

OBSESSION is for those readers. It is set in California, a place I have loved for many years. The story starts in Southern California and travels up the coast to San Francisco. It is a fast paced read that should keep you on the edge of your seat.

Enjoy!

Terence Munsey.

For

Samantha whom I love and will forever miss,

and

Clemintine and Winston,

dear old friends never to be forgotten.

God bless.

All I hear...all I touch...all I see...all I feel...all I dream...

Is... all I want.

●

Their car was traveling at a high speed. It was moving faster and faster as it weaved along and down the cliff road of the old coast highway. It was getting dark. The sun was just beginning to sink into the ocean. With each new turn they were going more out of control and picking up speed. Something was wrong. The wheels were shooting up gravel from the shoulder of the road with each nearly missed turn along the steep cliff roadway. Left. Right. Left. Straight. More speed. Brakes not working. Losing control. Then crashing through the side barrier and the long silent flight through the air in slow motion, till the bang of the impact upon the rocks of the ocean below...

She screams and awakens from this recurrent nightmare. It is as she imagines the crash must have been. She is shaken. In her desperation, she realizes that she must make a change and start a new life away from her past.

●

Chapter

THREE MONTHS LATER

A beat up old blue Chevy pulled up along the long narrow street and into the driveway of the stark brick building. Noisily it pulled up and parked in a lot that was fenced in from all sides. After a couple of seconds the engine stuttered to a halt. Then with a loud creak the driver's side door opened. Out into the morning sunlight, stepped a young slender woman. She was wearing a simple dress. It was summery and bright. In her right hand a large man's leather travel briefcase was carried . It was worn. It was beginning to burst at a couple of its seams and its original tan, was discolored with age and experiences.

As she opened her door and got out of the car, the young woman dropped a book onto the pavement. She fumbled as it fell, trying to prevent it from falling from her, but was too late. She bent down revealing her beautiful long legs, picked it up and then placed it under her left arm. She moved away from the door and bumping it with her behind, pushed the door closed. The door made a loud squeak and then a thud as it closed.

She walked across the parking lot and then hurried onto the path that led to the entrance of the building. She was late. The drive in had taken longer than she had anticipated. It was five after nine in the morning and her first day. It was Thursday and a short work week. She did not want to make the wrong impression.

Going as fast as she could, she arrived at the building and entered through the main doors. She knew where to go. She remembered from her interview of the previous month. Once past the entrance she turned left and walked into and down a long narrow hallway. It was a typical school hallway. She marveled at how little things changed. It was like going back in time to her own school days. The design was still the same. There were painted cinder blocks rising from the very old but highly polished marble-like speckled floor, to the ceiling, where a long row of discolored florescent lights glowed. There were lockers farther down on the left side. She thought to herself what a dismal place to have spend so much of her life.

As she continued down the hallway, she passed four classrooms. Everyone in each of the rooms was in their places and quietly working. She could tell by taking a quick look through the classroom door windows. No-one noticed nor said anything to her as she quickly made her way past and down to the end of the hall. She soon arrived at the very last door opposite the rear exit of the school. She had arrived at her own room. She paused a moment. She was a little nervous. She took in a deep breath, then opened the door and entered.

It was a tiny shoe box of a room, measuring no more than twelve feet by six. Almost what she expected a prison cell would be like.

'How typical.' she thought.

There was a large window directly opposite without curtains, which faced the street and the school front lawn and trees. To her immediate left there was a normal sized blackboard, but it was green, which covered the entire wall length of the room. It made the room feel smaller. Taking up most of the floor space was one large table placed centrally, with four wooden chairs neatly tucked under it. The room was otherwise empty and claustrophobic. No-one else had yet arrived.

She entered into the room and squeezed her way between the green board and table towards the window, where there was a narrow empty shelf above the radiator. She placed her briefcase upon the shelf, and after unfastening its clasp, pulled out her papers in preparation for the day's work. She looked very professional.

This was the first day at the new job, she wanted everything to go right. She found herself wondering, as she prepared, if she really wanted to be here; wondering if this was the right place for her to be. It was not exactly what she had expected her first 'real' teaching job to be like. She quickly shrugged these thoughts away. It was money. It was an opportunity that could not be passed. It was a foot in the door to her so far meager career.

After several minutes, she had all her papers laid out and organized on the large table, and was seated in one of the chairs. She now only needed the arrival of her students in order to begin her instruction. These were not the regular students that were attending throughout the rest of the building. She was part of a separate program. A program that used this tiny space and was offered jointly through Social Services and the Board of Education, but was completely disassociated with this school and its regular program. The physical space was the only distant connection. It was a school within a school. The students in her program were misfits, adults who had tried and never been able to complete the most fundamental elements of reading, writing, and arithmetic. The three R's. This was their one last chance before the system gave up on them. Her job was to teach these adults; to motivate them to improve their otherwise abusive lives. She recalled her interview and how she had felt like a missionary being appointed to her task of salvation. She had not commented on her observation. She needed the job.

She sat nervously waiting, as she wondered what type of human beings she was about to meet. She fixed her gaze upon the clock that was above the closed door. It was a typical school clock with its large black hands and numbering. She checked it against her wrist watch. Either her watch was eight minutes fast, or the school had its own control over time. It showed nine thirty AM.

"Where is everybody?" she said nervously out loud to herself in the empty room.

Just at that moment, there came a knocking at the door.

"Hello? Come in." she called out as she rose from her seat.

In came two long haired scruffy looking men. They appeared to be in their twenties. She thought that they might be street people and not students, who were wrongly in the building and in the inappropriate place. She was polite and cheery to them as they opened the door,

"Can I help you guys?"

"Ah…Yeah… We're here for…ah…We're here for the adult class."

"Oh. Yes… Come on in." she was taken aback but did not let it show, as she moved from her chair to properly greet them.

"My name's Monika," she held out her hand to guide them to the seats. "Monika Queller. Have a seat."

"Thanks very much." they each replied almost in unison as they came in and each found seats. The two men sat at the large bare table staring aimlessly at the green board directly in front of them. They seemed so out of place and dirty to

Monika.

Nothing more was said by them. They each waited. They for her to begin, and she for more late arrivals. After it was clear that no-one else was coming, she began the day's work. She did not want to put these two off by waiting too long for latecomers. She decided to start. Anyone who was late could catch up. She went through all the normal welcoming procedures: the introductions, instructions, outlines, demands, expectations. She could tell that these two were not here to learn, that other reasons for their attendance were involved. No matter what she did they were not very interested. She did not inquire into their reasons. She was happy enough to leave them alone and make it through this first day.

The morning passed slowly. Not being able to get much conversation or response from either of them, she assigned them much work. They were not pleased, and let her know this by indirect verbal complaint. She ignored their comments. She gave them notes. She gave them books. She explained ideas and encouraged them to participate. It was a grueling task. They were not at all cooperative. She quickly realized that this was going to be a difficult job. The day slowly passed.

No-one else ever entered during that day, neither student nor inquisitive person who was in the building. She felt ostracized, on her own, hidden in a silent, lonely corner of the school. Finally as the day ended, the two students rose as they were dismissed and spoke more than they had all day, saying good bye. After they left, she sat down to relax and contemplate the day. She hoped she would see them or at least someone the next day, although she did not expect it. She leaned back on the chair and placed her legs up to rest on the window sill. She looked out into the vast world beyond this very small room. Her 'school' finished about half an hour after the regular school day. There was no one else around. She felt a loneliness. She wondered if she had made the right choice in taking this job; if she had been smart about moving here and starting over.

Suddenly, and without warning the door to her room opened. It startled her. She lost her balance as she turned to see who it was and fell from the chair and onto the hard floor with a loud bang.

"Oh!...Are... Are you okay?...I'm sor...sorry. I...I did...I...I...didn't mean to..."

From the floor she looked up towards the person standing in the doorway. There was a tall, well-structured, good looking man. He was dressed in a dark suit that fit him nicely. He was in his early thirties. He had the most attracting green eyes that she had ever seen and was spell-bound momentarily by their pleasant sparkle. Everything about him felt instantly perfect. It was an odd sensation. By the way he was staring at her, she felt as if he knew her.

"No…No, no. That's fine. It's my fault. I…ah…I shouldn't have been…ah…sitting like that." she said as she tried to scramble to her feet. She felt embarrassed more at being a little flus-tered by this strange man than by her fall.

"Oh…" he looked back at her in an odd way, but that was all he said.

"Hi. I'm Monika." she offered her hand as she rose. He threw his hand out to meet hers. He walked closer and into the room to shake her hand. She took hold of his offered hand. She felt the firmness of his grip, as it surrounded her skin. "Monika. Monika Queller. Hi."

"Nice to meet you, Monika. Hi." he replied. There was life in his eyes. "So how was your first day?"

As he said this he observed the close quarters of the room. He noticed the mess from the papers that had fallen. Monika caught his observation and turned to pick them up. He quickly bent to help and they both collected them from the floor.

Monika continued talking as he helped her,

"Oh,… Yes…It went fine. Not many students, but…ah…I think it will be great."

She noticed his masculine scent as they finished picking up the papers. They stood and he gave the few remaining papers that he held to her.

"Well…If there's anything you need, I'm just down the hall. 1 0 5."

"1 0 5." she raised her eyes and tilted her head to physically indicate the direction.

"Yes, just a couple of doors down." he confirmed.

"Well…Thank you." she shrugged and smiled. He returned her smile.

"Okay. Good bye. Oh, by the way I'm James. James Anstey." he said as he lingered a moment before he turned and went through the doorway and into the hall.

"Good bye."

There was an awkward moment. She followed him to the doorway and watched for a moment as he walked away and into his classroom.

"Wow." she said under her breath as she re-entered her room and closed the door. "Now this is more like it. James Anstey."

Monika went over and placed the papers that they had picked up from the floor neatly into her large tan briefcase. The briefcase was very old. It had been her father's. It was all she had left to remind her of him. She leaned over to be comforted by the smell of the leather. How she missed him, she reminisced. It had been over seven months now. She continued tidying up.

Once all her books and papers were in place, she closed the briefcase and fastened it. She then picked it up by its ragged leather grip, and made her way out of the room. She closed the door behind her, and walked down the hall towards the entrance she had come through that morning. As she walked, she passed the same classrooms, but this time one of the doors was open. She continued on, the sound of her footsteps echoing throughout the hall. She came to the open door, 105 was written on it at eye level. She decided to peek in. It was a large standard classroom. James was sitting in the front of the room adjacent to the doorway at his desk. He was marking his papers.

"Hi again." she interrupted him from his work.

"Are you on your way out?" he did not mind her interruption.

"Yes, ah….I thought ah…I'd call it a day and go and get ready for tomorrow."

"Yeah. You're probably gonna need it. The second day is harder."

"Yeah." she agreed. There was a nice awkwardness between them. "Well…I'd better be on my way."

He half stood up from his desk and seemed to be about to say something, then changed his mind. "Ah… Well… Good bye again."

"Yeah." she smiled and backed awkwardly out of the doorway and on down the hall to the main entrance.

As she exited the school, she noticed a chill in the air. The weather had changed. Clouds were just beginning to move in and block the sun. It was overcast and felt like it was going to rain. She walked down the pathway to her car in the parking lot. As she neared the parking lot, she noticed that the windshield of her car appeared to be shattered, with a hole in it about six inches in diameter. It was easy to see that someone had smashed her car window during the day.

"Oh great." she complained as she dropped her briefcase and ran to the car to investigate. Upon a closer look, she saw that there was a large rock on the front seat of her car, which had obviously been thrown through the windshield.

"Dam idiots." she walked away and returned to her briefcase, picked it up and went angrily back towards the school. She would have to call the police. This was going to delay her here for quite a while. She was fuming as she walked back down the path into the building and directly into the main office. There was an older crabby looking woman, the secretary, sitting behind a high counter. Monika stood at the counter and waited. The secretary ignored her.

"Ah um." Monika cleared her throat. The secretary looked up.

"Yes."

"Hi. I'm Monika Queller, and I teach for the adult section."

"Oh yeah." she was nonchalant.

"Ah… My car. Someone's…ah someone's broken the windshield."

"Oh yeah." she was dispassionate in her tone.

"Can I use your phone?" Monika realized that there was no point wasting much time or energy on the secretary.

"Yeah. Use that one over there. Push number three, and then nine to get out."

"Thanks." Monika gave her a dirty look, but it had no effect. She crossed behind the counter and over to the phone and picked up the receiver. "Do you have a phone book?"

"Ah, over there in the top right hand drawer." the secretary pointed.

Monika followed her 'pointing' to the upper drawer and pulling it open revealed the phone book. She couldn't help but think how little things had changed since her day's in school. No wonder the kids dropped out as soon as they were of legal age. She opened the book and found the local police number and proceeded to dial. It rang three times.

"Fifteen Precinct, Sergeant Murray."

"Oh, hi. My name is Monika Queller. I want to report some vandalism to my car."

"Anyone hurt, Ma'am?" the Sergeant asked matter-of-factly.

"No. Just the windshield is smashed, and I want to report it."

"Okay Ma'am. I'll send a car over. It will be a while. I haven't got anyone available immediately."

"How long will that be?"

"A while. Sorry Ma'am, but if there's nobody hurt, you're just going to have to wait. It's the best we can do, Ma'am."

"Okay, fine. Here's the address." she gave the policeman the address and all other required details, then said good-bye and hung up. The secretary who had overheard everything, did not react. Monika turned and said,

"Thank you." and made her way along the counter.

"You're welcome, dear." the secretary's patronizing and insincere 'dear' irritated her but Monika did not outwardly react.

As she was leaving the office, James was leaving his classroom and coming down the hallway.

"You still here?" he called out.

"Yeah. Someone's damaged my car."

"Oh no. Really? Is it bad? Where?"

"In the lot. The windshield. Someone smashed the windshield."

"Can I help? Anything I can do?" He was now a few yards from her.

"I've just called the police, but they won't be here for a while. So I suppose I'll just have to wait till they show up. So much for an early night."

"Oh…Well…Okay. That might be a long time?" he was asking as he reached her.

"Yes."

They chatted as they walked out of the building and down the path to her car. They soon found themselves at the parking lot. James quickly saw the damage.

"Someone sure did a number on your car."

"Yeah, and on the first day."

"Well… It happens unfortunately. It's probably

some jerk."

"Yeah."

They both stood silently looking at the damage. James had an idea:

"Why don't you leave it here. When the police come they can write a report and you can get it from them later. Why don't you come with me and get some dinner? Unless you've got other plans?"

"No. I haven't any."

"Well. It's settled then."

She was tired, and she was hungry. The weather was changing and looking worse. She didn't like the idea of waiting around by herself until the police arrived—if they arrived. She felt uneasy that whomever had done the damage may still be nearby.

"Okay." she decided.

"Great." he said. He led her over to the other side of the lot to his car. It was a red Corvette. He walked around to the passenger side and opened the door for her.

"Thank you." she said as she got into the car and sat in the old black leather seat. He closed the door after her and then walked around to his side, unlocked the door and got in beside her.

"Well, what do you want to eat?" he asked as he

put the key into the ignition and started the engine.

"Anything's fine. Anything at all."

"I know a nice little place on the East side."

"That sounds fine. I live on the East side."

"Me too. Where?" he smiled as he backed up. They exchanged addresses.

As they were conversing, she couldn't help but thinking what a crazy day it had turned into. James was great. He had a warm sense of humor. His hair was short and he had a nice rugged face. His body was svelte. He obviously took care of himself. Matching the color of his suit, he was wearing a dark gray shirt and a tie that blended in beautifully. She felt her heart skip as she looked at him.

Their conversation continued without break all the way to the restaurant. They drove up and parked on the street directly in front. It was a Vietnamese restaurant. She had never been to a Vietnamese restaurant. From the outside it looked more like a cafeteria style than a formal style restaurant. He got out of the car and crossed to her side. He opened the car door for her.

"Thank you." she said as she got out.

"I hope you don't mind this place. It's not very formal. It's very casual, but they have the best

Pho Bun in town."

"Pho Bun?" she questioned.

"Noodle soup. It's their national food."

"Soup?"

"It's really more of a meal, like a stew. It has broth, meat, vegetables. You'll love it. If you're still hungry afterwards, we can go somewhere else, okay?"

"Oh, no, no, no. I'm sure it will be lovely." she was not sure at all, but his enthusiasm about the place intrigued her.

They went into the restaurant and were shown to a table. The room was very brightly lit. Not at all the romantic dinner she had fantasized it might be. They quickly sat, then James placed the order. Tea was brought. He poured. They sipped and chatted while they waited for the soup.

"So, when did you graduate?" he started the conversation on a more personal tone.

"Last year."

"Have you been teaching anywhere else?"

"I've done substitute teaching, night school, and odds and ends. Nothing permanent though. This is really my first full time job."

"That's great. It's going to be a hard job, but just remember," he placed his hand over hers, "if there's anything you need, I'm here."

"Thank you." her eyes met his.

The conversation turned to other topics, and it was not long before the soup was presented. One large bowl of soup was placed in the middle, and two smaller empty bowls in front of them. There were chopsticks and two ceramic spoons. He took a spoon and served some broth into her bowl, and then using a set of chopsticks, gave her some noodles, meat and vegetables. He then served himself.

"Any hot sauce?"

"No thank you. I'll try it like this first." she looked a little uneasy.

"Is there something wrong?" he asked.

"Well, ah... I've never used chopsticks before." she laughed embarrassingly.

"Really?"

"Really. I've always gone to the standard Chinese restaurants and used fork and knife."

"Oh. Here. It's easy. Let me help you."

He leaned over and showed her how to hold the sticks. They laughed as more food fell back into the bowl than into her mouth. They were having a nice time, and though she did not eat much, she was enjoying the outing. It was fun. It had been so long since she could remember feeling so comfortable. He was so easy to talk to. He was friendly, kind and sensitive. She felt as if she had known him all her life, and not just a few hours.

When they had finally finished the meal, he asked if she would like anything else.

"No. Thank you. You were right. That was great. Besides I had better get going. I have a lot to do tomorrow."

"Okay."

James called the waiter over, and paid the bill. It was time to go. They both rose. James left a tip on the table. As they left the restaurant the waiter said good-bye. It was a friendly place. As they left the restaurant, James took Monika's hand and escorted her to the car and again opened the passenger door. Monika got in and James went around and into his side. He started the car and put on its headlights. It was just getting dark.

As the car pulled out, she gave James the directions to her home.

●

It did not take long to get to Monika's house. In minutes they were there. James pulled the car to the curb in front of her house.

"Well, good night." The car was still running. He jumped out and ran to her side, and opened the door.

"Thanks. I had a great time. See you tomorrow."

she said as she got out of the car with her brief-case.

"Eight o'clock?" he said.

"Tomorrow?" she did not understand.

"You're car. I can come by this way and pick you up in the morning, if you'd like?"

"Oh—okay. Are you sure it isn't out of your way?"

"Not at all. I have to come by this way anyway."

She gave him a light kiss on his right cheek, and then made her way to her front door. He got back into the car and watched while she found her key and opened the door. She smiled and waved good-bye. He waved back and drove off into the night. As she entered and closed the door, she leaned with her back upon it for support,

"This is going to be a great job."

She dropped her briefcase, and went to the phone to call the police about her car. There was no point in returning to it tonight. She would call her insurance company in the morning from school, and arrange to have it fixed during the day if that was possible. She was not worried about any further damage. It was an old clunker as far as she was concerned. It was nice to drive a car like that in the city.

She did not know that other eyes were watching

her, following her, scrutinizing her from a distance since the beginning of this day. They were hidden eyes. They stalked her every movement. She could go nowhere without them. They were waiting and watching for the right time.

Chapter

B ZZZZZZZZZZZZZZZZZZZZZZZZZZZZZZZZZZZZZ zzzzz! The startling tone of the alarm sounded: seven o'clock AM. The sun was rising and brightly shining through her windows. The room was decorated in off-white tones. Taking up the central position in front of the windows was a large four poster bed made of pine. It was very soft and welcoming. Part of the bed was covered with a large down comforter which was draped over it, then partially across her and onto the hardwood floor. The bay windows had a sheer curtain which was billowing in the light breeze of morning. The windows overlooked the street from the second story of her home.

Monika gradually roused as the noise penetrated her sleep. Only a light sheet remained protecting her delicate skin. She had kicked most of the comforter off during the warmth of the night. Her strawberry blond hair was ruffled over her pillow. She was faced down.

Bzzzzzzzzzzzzzzzzzzzzzzzzzzzzzzzzzzzzzzzzzzzzzzzzzzzz zzzzzzzzzzzzzzzzzzzzz!

The constancy of the alarm was annoying. Reflexively her left arm moved from under the sheet and towards the alarm clock without her visual assistance, in an effort to find the button that would stop the noise. She lifted her head to the left and with sleepy eyes found the clock. Seven AM. Guided by her sight, she stretched her hand over to the button, turning the buzzing off.

"Oooohhh." she moaned as she slowly came to life. She rolled over and onto her back, sinking into the fluffy mattress. The sheet fell lower revealing her breasts.

"Oooohhh." she stretched and yawned again as she sat up.

Kicking back the sheet, she placed her hands behind her and onto the bed to support her as she slid her slender legs over the side placing her feet firmly upon the floor. She then raised her arms above her head and stretched once more as she stood up. Every curve of her was exposed to view. She looked out of the window to the rising morning sun. It was to be another beautiful California day. She turned away from the scene and crossed the room to the bedroom door, opened it, and went down the short hall to the bathroom, which was at the top of the staircase that led from the main floor below to the second. She opened the door and entered, closing it behind her.

It was a small, simple, but modern bathroom. Monika stood in front of the mirror that was above a marble sink and counter. Leaning forward she said,

"Good morning," to herself.

She moved to the shower stall which was adjacent to the sink and opened its hinged glass doors. Leaning in, she began to adjust the taps, feeling the water as it poured from the main spout. She tried to keep out of reach of the splashing cold water as it cascaded off the inside shower walls and floor. She placed one hand amidst the flow. It was very cold. When the temperature blend was correct, she pushed in the controlling knob and the shower sprang to life. She quickly pulled back out of its way. Water was now beginning to spray more strongly onto the bathroom floor. Carefully she stepped into the shower stall and closed the door. The opaqueness of the glass partially concealed the definition of her as she began to wash. The soft touch of her fingers upon her skin through the delicate lather of the soap, caressed her. She started to hum a tune.

After several minutes the sound of the spraying water stopped. She opened the door and grabbed for a fluffy white towel on the rack opposite the wall to the sink. She dried herself in the stall, then stepped from the shower into the bathroom, closing the shower door behind her. She wrapped the large towel around her, securing it in place by tucking in one part between her bosom and the wrapped towel. Then, picking up another smaller towel from the same rack, proceeded to dry her hair. When she had finished, she wrapped this towel around her head like a turban.

Now that she was dry and snugly wrapped, she exited the bathroom. She walked down the hall and back to her room to her closet to decide what she would wear today. She felt happy. She had only just met him and wondered at her sudden elation in the anticipation of his picking her up. This thought predominated as she searched through her clothes. She pondered over what would be best and finally picked a light cotton dress.

"That's the one." she said as she pulled it from the closet and lay it on her bed.

Crossing over to her dresser, she undid her body towel and let it fall to the floor. She opened the second drawer and chose her standard cotton panties, then changed her mind and selected a more delicate bra and panties. She put them on and then walked back across the room through the bedroom door and back to the bathroom, to finish her hair and put on her make-up.

After fifteen minutes she returned to her room and put on her dress. The turban was now removed from her head and her damp hair was combed; it would be dry by the time she left the house. She then turned to the bed and quickly threw the covers from the floor back over the mattress and made the room appear a little more neat. Satisfied with her clean up, she left her room to go downstairs and put on some coffee. This was her usual breakfast.

The kitchen was cozy and in the back of the house on the lower main level directly opposite the front doors and down a narrow hallway. Through its several large windows could be seen a small but plush garden. She had made her way here, made the coffee, and was now sitting at a round white table. Her elbows were upon the table top supporting her double grip of a mug of coffee as she sipped. Still not completely awake, Monika was lost in thought and gazing into the beauty of the garden through the large windows.

She was thinking of the day ahead...and James. She noticed the counter clock in the kitchen. It was twenty to eight. It was getting late. She rushed herself. He would be here soon and she did not want to keep him waiting.

Taking one last gulp from her mug, she stood and placed it in the sink. She would wash it later. She turned and exited, going down the hall to the front doorway where her briefcase lay sitting untouched from the night before, where she had left it. She went to the front door and drawing back its small quarter curtain, peered out onto the front path and street.

He was not there. She considered whether she should wait inside for him, or go out down the path and wait for him by the street. She felt uneasy. Somehow in her mind, she was not will-ing or ready to invite him into her home. She wanted a little more time before she took that step. More time to understand the suddenness of her feelings. It was so unlike her to be thinking this way so soon after meeting James.

She had been alone for over seven months, having finally ended a relationship that had not worked out to her liking. It had upset her, and she was not sure she was ready or that she wanted to be in another relationship.

She wanted this situation with James to go slowly, but she knew inside that it was beyond her rational control. It was so unusual and fast for her to be interested so quickly in someone. It seemed unbelievable to her, but it was happening. She was already beginning to care for him. She attributed this rapid interest to the acute loneliness she had felt over the past few months.

Picking up her keys from a brass dish which lay on the small entrance table, and grabbing her briefcase, she opened the door. She had decided. As she left, she pulled the door. It locked automatically as it shut. She was invigorated. The sun was already warm. It was going to be a hot day in many ways. She followed the short walkway to the sidewalk, where she placed her briefcase on the pavement and stood waiting.

After a few minutes of waiting, Monika realized that she did not remember the make of James' car. She did recall however, the color and that it was sporty. All her life she had never paid much attention to makes of cars, and in the upset of the previous day, she had neglected to pay much attention to James'. She was embarrassed and slightly panicked. She checked the time on her wrist watch: five minutes to eight. The street was getting busier with people and traffic. Suddenly she was startled by a car horn honking. She looked up as a red Corvette pulled up to the curb. It was James. He leaned over to unlatch the door from the inside. The road was busy and he would not be able to stop long.

"Hi. Good morning. Get in." he did not give her a chance to answer.

Monika picked up her briefcase, fully opened the door and jumped into the car. Once securely in, and with the door closed, she replied,

"Good morning. Right on time."

They both exchanged smiles and he pulled out into the traffic. She noted that he was even better looking than she remembered from the night before.

The drive this morning seemed slower than the previous evening. This was in part due to the volume of the rush hour traffic. They drove on in silence for a little way, until James had pulled off from the side streets and onto the freeway. Once he had safely maneuvered into the main lanes and was solidly in the flow of cars, he broke their awkward silence,

"It's like this every day," he indicated the cars with a nod of his head and a motion of his right hand, as his left held onto the steering wheel. It was stop and go traffic. "I've never liked commuting, but it's all I've ever done," he chuckled. "One day I'm just going to find a job away from here…all this, and stop the nonsense. It's crazy. I'm crazy." he was trying to get the conversation going.

She paid attention but did not respond. He continued,

"It's pretty aggravating, but I 'spose if I wasn't doing this, I'd start to miss the aggravation." he laughed at the irony.

She smiled and laughed with him.

"How long have you been there?" Monika inquired.

"There? School?"

"Yes,"

"Five years. It's been good, and don't get me wrong, I like it. It's just this…this commuting. It takes all the fun away."

"Well, maybe one day you, you never know, you might find a nice place…and get away from all this. I hope to."

"Well. One day…" He looked at her. "It would be nice to settle down…get a white picket fence…a family…out of the rat race…"

"What about the house." They both laughed as they imagined living away from the city and surrounded by the fence, but no house.

"One day." James replied.

They laughed at the idea as their attention went back to the traffic and the commute. Monika was musing about the image of the white picket fence, a cozy country home and family. How warm and lovely the idea was in the right circumstances. On they drove in silence as they both daydreamed not realizing that they were both thinking the same thoughts.

They continued off and on with small talk as they commuted. Soon they came to their exit. James signaled and pulled off the freeway to the roadway that led to the school. The whole trip had taken thirty five minutes from Monika's house to the off ramp. In another ten minutes they would be at work.

It was so comfortable in the car with James. Monika felt as if she had known him for years. She could tell that he also enjoyed the company and the ride with her. They drove on in silence and soon came within sight of the school. As they approached, James noted,

"Oh. There's something going on. Look."

"Where?" Monika stretched up and looked forward.

"There," James pointed ahead and to his left. "In the school parking lot."

"Oh…yeah." she now saw the place. There were many cars in the small school lot and a crowd of people gathered around talking and watching. There was a police car parked in the driveway of the lot. James slowly pulled past the police car and into the lot. He had to drive carefully to get by the crowd. He rolled down his window and asked one of his colleagues who was nearby,

"Hey…Hey Bill. What's going on here?"

"Looks like we've had some pretty bad vandalism done to one of the cars. It's pretty well totaled. We're not sure who's it is."

"Oh…oh…" James tried to see through the people, but it was difficult at his seated level. He pulled the car forward and into a parking spot. Both he and Monika opened their doors and got out to get a better look.

"My car!" Monika was shocked as she saw the sight before her. "Look. It's my car."

James' eye was led by Monika's pointing right

hand. Her blue Chevy had been vandalized. Not only was the windshield broken, but every window and glass object was smashed. There was a shower of shattered glass everywhere. There was also black and silver spray paint of graffiti all over the surface of the vehicle. All four tires were slashed and flat. It looked like an abandoned wreck. There were two policemen standing in front of it. One was writing notes while the other was taping off the area with yellow 'DO NOT CROSS' ribbon.

Monika hurried over towards the officer who was taking notes.

"My car. Wha… What happened to my car?!"

"Ma'am." The officer looked up from his notes. "Is this yours?"

"Yes… This, is my car!?" Monika was shaking her head as she answered.

"Ma'am. I'm Detective Atero. When did you park it here?"

"Yesterday…ahm… In the morning… Last night…It was here all day. Someone smashed the windshield and I left it here. I called… I called you…You were meant to come and do a report." Monika was too upset to register his name in her mind.

"Yes, Ma'am. A report was made, and it was all

done by the night shift. We got the call this morning, here, because there was trouble, and …ah…this is what we found."

"Called? By whom?"

The officer checked his notes.

"A Ms. Wembly. The school secretary."

"What happened? Who did this?" Monika was only half listening.

"We were hoping you could help us find out. We don't know Ma'am. This is how we found it about fifteen minutes ago. How long have you been working here?" The officer changed the subject and began his investigation.

"This is my second day."

"Do you have any enemies that you know of? Anyone who might have done this?"

"Enemies?" A realization struck home. "I don't understand."

"It's a little unusual for someone in their first couple of days at a job to have a perfect stranger do this type of damage. Perpetrators usually are getting even with, say a teacher they dislike. But after only two days…"

"I don't understand." Monika was stunned by the damage and the implication of what the officer was saying. As she stood listening to the officer, James had followed after and walked up next to her.

"What a mess. We've never had this happen."

"Sir." the officer acknowledged James' comment. "Are you…?"

"James Anstey. I work here." as he answered, he moved to comfort Monika. They all stood viewing the vehicle. The officer interrupted,

"Well, there really isn't too much that we can do right now, but we'll check out whatever leads we can find." he was talking to Monika, "Have you got time to answer a few more questions? We will need some more details."

Monika came out of her stupor. "Yeah. Just let me get things set and organized here and ah…get someone to take my class. Then we can talk."

"That's fine. I'll be here."

"Who could have done this? Why?" Monika spoke her thoughts out loud. No one answered. She then turned and with James, walked away to the path which led on to the school. They walked down the path and entered the building by the main entrance. As they passed the office and began to go down the hall Ms. Wembly called out to her from inside the office,

"Miss. Queller. Miss. Queller."

"Yes?" Monika responded in an irritated manner.

"Call for you on line two. Oh…sorry about your car, but you shouldn't leave it in the lot over night." she was matter-of-fact, not rude.

"Thank you. Where can I take it?" Though Monika was annoyed by the bluntness of Ms. Wembly, she did not feel the inclination to deal with it. She ignored it.

"Right in here, dear." Ms. Wembly was sarcastic.

Monika with James, went back and into the office. Ms. Wembly was again seated behind her desk.

"There. Use that one." she indicated the same phone as yesterday.

Monika walked over, and pausing before she lifted the receiver, took in a deep breath to compose herself. Then grabbing the receiver, lifted it up to her right ear and depressed the flashing button on the base of the phone.

"Hello. Monika Queller speaking." she awaited a response but there was nothing. "Hello? Hello." There was still no reply. She was about to take the receiver from her ear and hang up when she heard a man's voice,

"We want it."

"Hello? Who is this?"

"We want it."

There was a click, and the line went dead.

"Hello? Hello!? Who is this? Hello. Hello."

She pulled the receiver away, and looked up to James who, having overheard Monika's voice, was concerned by the odd conversation.

"What was that all about?" he asked.

"Ah...I don't know. Some...Some man. He wanted something. I don't...I...I...don't...It must have been a wrong number." Monika then directed a question to the secretary. "Who did they ask for?" She meant the caller.

"Monika Queller."

"By name, exactly?"

"Yes. He asked if Monika Queller worked here, and could he speak with you."

"What did the man sound like?"

"Just a normal man's voice. What's wrong dear?"

"I don't know. It was really strange. This is all pretty strange. It's a great way to start my second day."

They all looked to one another. Monika shrugged it off. So much had happened this morning. She would not let this prank call bother her now, though she did appear to James to be upset.

"Look, Monika." James started. "I have a first period spare. I'll take your class. Why don't you go talk to the police and get this all dealt with right away."

"Are you sure?"

"Yes, no problem. Go ahead. See if you can make any sense out of all this."

"Thank you James. I have some work here you can give them. It will keep them busy till I come back." Monika put her old briefcase up on the counter and opened it. She pulled out a few papers to give to James. "I haven't photocopied them yet. Would you mind making five or six copies and then give it to them and just work through it?"

"Sure. No problem. Let me have the papers."

She passed the papers over to James. She then closed her briefcase, and picking it up, hurriedly left the office. She went across the hall and out of the main entrance. Once outside she hurried down the path to the school parking lot and the police. There was still a crowd standing around.

In the office James turned to Ms. Wembly after Monika had left.

"What do you make of all this?"

"It's beyond me Mr. Anstey. A lot of strange types are running around loose out there."

"Yeah." His mind went to thought as the secretary nattered on. Ms. Wembly was the most ornery person he had ever encountered. He did not hear her words. There was something very odd going on here.

In the parking lot, Monika was talking with a police officer. He was scribbling down notes as they conversed. He was asking all the routine questions required under the circumstances: name, address, family, background, trying to find something that could be a lead, or reason for the vandalism.

"Now, can you think of anybody who might have done this? Someone you've had a recent argument with? An enemy? Someone who doesn't like you?"

"No. No-one. Nothing like this has ever happened to me before."

"Well," the officer was at a loss. "I don't know what we can do, ah…Phone your insurance company, and give them my name."

He pulled from his pocket a small white card with dark blue printing and presented it to Monika.

"Thank you." She took it and looked at it subconsciously. "Detective John Atero. If I think of anything, I'll let you know." This time his name registered.

"Okay. Sorry about all this." He closed his notebook, and took another look at the car. "I hope we can find out who did this, but frankly Ma'am, it's not very likely."

They both looked at the car with its graffiti painted exterior, smashed windows and torn seats.

"Whoever this was, it was more than just vandalism. They were looking for something."

"Looking for what? I don't have anything." Monika became alarmed.

"I don't know Ma'am, but my instincts tell me there's something more to all this.

"More? More what?" She was worried at the possible ramifications.

"Oh…I don't mean to worry you, Ma'am." he noted her change of mood, "But is there any one you could stay with for a couple of days, just to be on the safe side? Till we can sort this out a bit more?"

"Stay with? Why? You think I'm in danger?"

"No, I'm sure it's nothing. Just someone to keep you company. A pretty girl like you …and all this…" he was trying to be diplomatic, "Just in case."

"No. All of my family are up north. I just moved here."

"That's fine then. Don't worry. I'm sure nothing more will come of this. Just routine." he meant his cautionary suggestion. "If you need anything, call."

"Thank you." Monika was perplexed.

The Detective stepped away and back to his car. Monika stood thinking.

"Who could have done such a thing? Why me? What were they looking for?" This was all so 'cloak and dagger'. She would drive herself crazy with these thoughts.

She mentally shook herself and turned away. She had work to do and students waiting. She walked back down the path, briefcase in hand and into the school. She made her way down the hallway that led to her classroom. Soon she was in front of it and after knocking gently, opened the classroom door. What a start to her day.

"Ms. Queller." James, who was sitting by the window while two students were working at the large table, stood. This drew the eyes of the same two male students from yesterday. They said good morning. She acknowledged them.

"Is everything okay?" James coming over, asked.

"Yes...Yes...but I won't be driving for a little while." she smiled.

"Did you speak to your insurance company?"

"No not yet. I wanted to check here first. To see

if everything was okay."

"Everything's fine. Go ahead. We're working hard." he was being sarcastic, but only Monika understood. "Make your calls. We'll be fine."

"Thank you." Monika exited, and made her way down the hall to the office to use the phone.

As she arrived and stepped into the office she asked of Ms. Wembly,

"Do you mind if I use the phone again?"

"Go ahead, dear. Just use the same one over there. Line two." Ms. Wembly was just as cold as before.

"Thank you." She went to the phone and put her briefcase upon the desk and opened it. She needed her address book for the phone number of her insurance company.

She picked up the phone and dialed the number. It was answered by a receptionist and directed to the claims department. She spoke for several minutes in an agitated way to an agent. After all the information had been exchanged, she said good-bye and hung up the phone.

"Thanks." she directed to Ms. Wembly as she picked up her briefcase and left to return to her classroom. First period was almost over.

Arriving again at her classroom door she repeated the knocking and opening as ten minutes before. Monika walked into the room,

"Thank you Mr. Anstey. Everything's taken care of."

"No problem at all. Anytime." James got up and crossed to the classroom door. As he came to her he put his left hand on her shoulder in a comforting way. "Let's meet over lunch. I think you need a friend."

"I'd like that."

"Good. I'll see you in a while then. Meet me outside the main entrance. We can walk down to the deli and get something light."

"Okay."

James left the room with a smile on his face. Monika, aware of her male students watching, quickly hid any emotion and became professional, getting back into the mind set of her job. So much had happened and it was just after ten AM. She was still obviously unsettled by all of the events of the morning, but her two male students did not say a word. They continued to do the work that had been given to them by James.

●

The morning went by quickly. Before she knew it, it was lunch time. She dismissed the students, telling them to come back at one thirty. They rose, leaving their work on the desk, and left without word to have lunch and a smoke. A few minutes later Monika also left the room. There was no bell. She walked down the hallway which was now full of young students going to their lockers and lunch. At the far end of the hallway, she saw James waiting for her by the school entrance. As she neared, he shouted hello and waved. She was soon standing in front of him.

"How was the rest of your morning?" James asked.

"Okay. No more problems."

"Is the deli alright?"

"Yeah… That sounds great."

"Let's go then."

He escorted her out of the building. They walked down the central path and turned right at the road that would lead to the deli. It was about two hundred yards down the street. They chatted as they walked.

They speedily arrived and went in to stand at the glass counter and place their order. It was a quaint New York style deli. It was busy and noisy with the preparation of the various sandwiches that were being ordered. All of the staff wore white shirts with the logo of the deli on front. A large man from behind the counter took their order. He was the owner, originally from Long Island.

James knew him well.

"Hi James. How are ya today."

"Fine Carlo. Meet a new colleague. Monika Queller."

"Things are looking up at the old factory." Carlo was obvious about his compliment as he smiled flirtatiously.

Monika smiled, "Hi."

"Pastrami on dark?"

"Yes. Make two." James answered, and then confirmed with Monika. "Is that alright?"

"Yes. That will be fine." Monika agreed.

Carlo wrote the order and called it out to his son who was buttering bread adjacent to him. His son repeated the order. It was a fun environment. Carlo then told them,

"Get a table before the rush. I'll bring your order over. Coffee?"

James looked to Monika. She accepted by nodding.

"Two. Regular." James ordered as they walked away from the counter and found a quaint table near the window. He helped Monika to her seat. James sat and began speaking,

"You've been having a very busy couple of days here."

"Yes. You could say that. I'd be happy with just

average and boring."

"What about your insurance?"

"They're going to send a tow truck over and take it into a local garage. After the mechanics look at it, my agent said he will call and let me know whether they will fix the car or write it off."

"Oh. When do you think you'll know?"

"He said they would tow it right away. Sometime after lunch."

"Well…I don't mean to push myself on you, but if you need a ride again…?"

"Oh…ah…ah…That's…That's such an imposition…"

"No, no. I am going your way anyway. Taking the bus is really not something you want to do if you have a choice."

"No…" she chuckled. "No. Although I don't know what else could happen to me now. What could be worse than what's already happened?"

"Yes. You're quite a veteran now. Welcome to Oceanside. It's a great welcoming."

"Thank you." Monika played along with the jovial mood. "I think someone's trying to tell me something."

"No. You know this isn't the typical behavior here. I've never had any problems before, and I'm sure nothing else is going to happen again."

"I hope you're right."

They both continued talking, and when their lunch arrived, they thanked Carlo, and began to eat. Their conversation changed to other topics as they lunched. They began to tell more personal aspects of their lives: family, brothers, sisters. All of James' family was in the area, but Monika was an only child. Her father had been a professor of physics at Stanford –the farm– but had mysteriously died with her mother in San Francisco last year. It was a car accident. Their bodies were never found, though their car was pulled from the ocean where it had crashed. It was a horrible time in her life. That was why she had left and come south. She had to get away from all the memories. To start over, afresh. James listened sympathetically as Monika spoke.

The time went quickly. Soon they had finished their lunch and verbal intercourse. James asked,

"Would you like anything else?"

"No. Thank you. That was great."

James looked at his wristwatch,

"It's about that time. Shall we leave?"

"Yes, but let me pay for this?"

"No. It isn't much, and I did ask you."

"I know but…"

"Next time you can get it."

"Are you sure?"

"Yes."

"Well…thank you."

They both rose. James went to the cash register to pay as Monika waited by the door. After paying, James went back to their table and placed a tip upon it. He then returned to Monika and together they left the deli to the sound of good byes and thank you's. Carlo watched after them when they had gone. Monika had made a lasting impression.

As the time was getting late, they both walked more quickly back to the school. Before they parted to return to their afternoon classes, they made arrangements to meet at the end of the day. They said their good-byes, and went on to their duties.

●

At three fifteen, when Monika finished her day, she left her classroom after dismissing her two students, and walked down the hallway to the office. She would check her mail box before leaving for the day. The memory of the strange phone call that morning returned to her as she entered the office. She was anxious. She went to check her mail box. There was nothing in the box. She felt relieved and decided that the call had been simply a prank. Ms. Wembly was still behind her desk as Monika turned to leave.

"See you tomorrow." Monika was polite to the secretary.

"See you tomorrow, dear."

Holding her briefcase firmly in her left hand, Monika walked out of the office and through the main entrance and down the path to the parking lot. James was standing by his car waiting. Monika visually scanned for her own car. It was no longer in the lot. It had been towed away. A glistening of the few remaining pieces of shattered glass that had been missed by the caretaker, whom she assumed swept up the mess, was the only hint that the old blue Chevy had been parked there.

"They must have come after lunch." James spoke out as Monika approached.

"Yeah." Monika shook her head in acknowledgment as she answered.

"Well. Hop in!" James opened the passenger door and escorted her in. "You must be anxious to get home and relax."

Monika got in. James closed her door and went around to the other side. He got in and put the key in the ignition and started the engine. Putting the car in reverse, he slowly backed out and maneuvered the car so that he could drive off.

Out of the lot they went, turning back onto the road, en route to the freeway. Monika did not speak on the return trip. She was distant. James said nothing. He understood. He left her to her thoughts.

●

The journey passed quickly. Before she had realized it, James had pulled up to the curb in front of her home.

"Well… You're home." he finally broke through.

"Oh…ah. Thank you…" Monika felt bad. She had not meant to ignore him. She had been uncommunicative and rude. "I…ah…I'm sorry. I didn't mean to be so rude. It's just been a hectic day…"

"No… I understand. You're entitled. Here." James took out a piece of paper and a pen from his pocket. He scribbled down something. "This is my phone number. If you need anything, or just want to talk, call. Okay?"

"Thank you." Monika smiled. It was so kind of him to offer. She had no other close friends in the vicinity. It was nice to know there was someone out there that she could call upon if need be.

"Would you like me to pick you up tomorrow?" There was a pause.

"Yes. You'd better have my number. It's 555-3236." James placed it in his memory as Monika continued: "Let me make all of this up to you somehow?"

"There's no need. It's nice to be able to help you out. Your company is payment enough."

"Well, thank you for everything." she indicated the number on the piece of paper which she held waving between the thumb and finger of her right hand.

"You're welcome."

She opened the door and got out. Before she closed the door, she leaned over, partially revealing herself through her low cut neckline,

"Remember, next meal is on me."

"Deal." James smiled. His eyes went from her soft looking skin to her sparkling eyes.

Monika closed the door and walked half way up the path to her front door. She turned and waved as James pulled away and disappeared into the traffic. She was feeling happy. She turned and continued up the path.

Arriving at the front door of her home, she put her briefcase down, knelt, opened it and searched for her keys. Finding them, she rose up to unlock the door. As she was about to insert the key, she noticed that the door was slightly ajar and the wood frame around the lock splintered, as if a crow bar had been prying between the frame and the locking mechanism. Lightly, Monika pushed the door with the fingers of her left hand. The door swung open a little more. Leaning carefully forward, she tried to peak through the open area into the house, expecting that there might be an intruder inside. She was scared. Not seeing anyone, she carefully and quietly pushed the door open enough to allow her to stealthily enter. Her key was tightly in her grip and exposed like a small knife blade. It was her only weapon.

She went into the main hallway. The place was a mess. It looked as if a tornado had struck. Everything was strewn everywhere. She became more afraid. Her heart was pounding and she was slightly out of breath. She wiped away a bead of sweat from her forehead, as she carefully proceeded deeper. She cautiously peaked into the living room area. It was a mess. She went down the hall into the kitchen. It was a mess. She wondered if anyone was here. If anyone was hiding. She walked back down the hall and stopped at the stairs. She held her breath as she listened to find out if there was anyone upstairs. She heard nothing. She decided to go up and make sure. She thought about getting a better weapon than the key in her hand. She looked around the immediate area. There was a broken metal lamp lying on the floor. She stooped and picked it up, wrapping the wire around the stand and grabbing hold of it at the end where the light bulb went. Wielding it before her, she crept up the stairs trying to avoid making any noise that would alert anyone upstairs to her presence. She wanted to keep the element of surprise on her side. Up she traveled step by step, all her instinctive senses primitively heightened.

When she had made it to the top, she began her search. She slowly walked down the hall to the bathroom, ready to pounce upon anyone she might meet. She entered the room. Nothing but a mess. She did not remain in the bathroom long. She left and went down the hall to her room. The door was closed. In one swift motion she threw the door open and yelled as she burst in. No-one was there, and again there was nothing but a mess. Everything was turned upside down. Monika breathed a sigh of relief. She sensed that whoever had done all of this was long gone.

Putting down the lamp on the disheveled bed, which was all pulled apart, Monika sat down. She was emotionally drawn. She tried to relax, then understood what she had to do. She got up and hurried downstairs to her briefcase which was at the front door. She rifled through it and found the card of the police detective she had met that morning, as well as the piece of paper with James' phone number. She then looked for the phone. After several moments she found it, and dialed the first number. It rang three times.

"Fifteenth Precinct." came the response.

"Detective Atero please."

"Yes Ma'am." she was put on hold for a moment.

"Atero."

"This is Monika Queller. We met this morning." her voice was shaky.

"Oh yes Ms. Queller. What can I do for you?" he could sense that she was upset by the tone of her voice.

"I've just come home, and everything is a mess. Someone has broken in! Everything's all over the place."

There was a pause at the other end of the line.

"Are you alone?"

"Yes."

"Call a friend to come over until we arrive. I'll be right there. Don't touch anything." The phone hung up with a click.

Monika read the number on the piece of paper

that James had just given her, then dialed the number. The phone rang four times and was answered by a machine,

"Hi. After the tone please leave your name and message." It was James' voice.

"Hi…James. This is Monika. I've been burglarized. I've called the police, but could you come …" before she could say more the line went dead. She tried to dial again, but there was no tone. Someone had cut the line. Someone was here! The phone was dead. She panicked. She thought she heard someone coming from the kitchen. No maybe it was coming from outside. She wasn't sure. Her instinct took over. She must hide. She could not go outside as it was not safe. She was flustered and wasn't sure where she should go. Out of reflex, she quickly turned and ran up the stairs and into her bedroom. She looked around for a place to hide. Instinctually she ran over to her closet, opened its louvered door and after closing the door behind her, went in behind the clothes squeezing into its deepest corner. It was the only place she felt secure. All she could do now was wait. She hoped the police or James would get there soon. She was terrified.

It was not long before the sound of footsteps reached Monika's ears. She was crouched up and afraid. With difficulty she stopped herself from making any noises. She waited, hoping that whoever it was, would go away. She was shaking with nervousness. She wanted to scream out, but did not. The footsteps were coming up the stairs. They were coming for her! They came down the hallway and stopped. She prayed for them to go. But they did not. They started again. They were coming closer. They entered into her room and stopped, again. Monika wanted to explode with fear, but found the wherewithal to remain silent. The steps resumed and came closer.

"Hello?" It was a familiar voice calling out to her, but paralyzed with fear and uncertainty, she did not respond. It was a man. She could not see him. She did not try. She stayed hidden.

The man was in his late twenties. He had longish blond hair, muscular build, and striking blue eyes. He was wearing blue jeans, a black T shirt, and steal tipped black snake skin cowboy boots. He paused and looked around. After several moments he turned, and walked out of the room and down the hall.

Frozen with apprehension, Monika listened as the footsteps gradually faded away down the stairs and out of the house. She was safe for the moment.

Chapter

B y the time James arrived home he was tired. It had been an eventful day. After parking his car, he slowly inspected his property and when satisfied that all was normal, found his way into his small adobe bungalow. He made his way into the living room and plopped himself down on the cozy soft divan. The room was small but beautifully furnished. The divan took up most of the space. An expensive television was off against the far wall about ten feet away. A glass coffee table, cluttered with magazines, was directly in front of the divan. The house was not very tidy or large, but it was comfortable; more comfortable than a teacher's salary could afford. James slouched back after picking up the TV remote from amongst the clutter of the table; put his feet upon the glass; turned the TV on, and began to relax. He leaned back and closed his eyes. It was good to be home.

Just as James was relaxing, the phone rang. He decided to let the answering machine take the message.

"Hi. After the tone please leave your name and message." It was James' voice. Then came the beep tone. James listened,

"We know your girlfriend has what we want. Tell her to…"

It was a man's voice. James was startled. He quickly shot up and got to the phone, which was a few feet away on the other side of the room. He picked up the receiver and a loud squeal sounded from the answering machine.

"Hello? Hello?" The squeal ended and James heard the click of the caller as he disconnected his phone from completing the call. "Hello?" There was nothing but the dial tone.

James hung up the phone. He was troubled by the call. He decided to play back the part of the message that the answering machine had recorded, just in case he could recognize the voice. He turned his attention to his answering machine, which indicated by a red light that there was a message. He pushed the rewind button. After several seconds the machine had rewound and begun to playback.

"James…Bill. Give me a call tonight." was the first message.

"Mr. Anstey, it's the Mission Book Shop. The books you ordered are in. Please come by and pick them up. Thank you." came the next message.

"Hi…James. This is Monika. I've been burglarized. I've called the police, but could you come …" before she could say more the line went dead.

Then the next message,

"We know your girlfriend has what we want. Tell her to…" It was the call that had just come in.

James quickly pushed the rewind button and as the tape rewound he could hear the voice speaking in a higher pitch and backwards. He stopped the machine just before the beginning of the message from Monika,

"…by and pick them up. Thank you."

"Hi…James. This is Monika. I've been burglarized. I've called the police, but could you come …"

James heard the fright in Monika's voice. He searched his memory for her phone number. Remembering it, he picked up the phone and quickly punched the numbers. The numbers connected but there was no sound.

"We know your girlfriend has what we want. Tell her to..." While James attempted to call Monika, the answering machine continued and played this last message before shutting off.

James became worried. There was no response on the phone line—nothing. The line was dead. Something was wrong. He decided he must go over to Monika's and see what was up.

Hanging up his phone, James left the living room and hurried out of the house to his car. He slid into the driver's seat and fumbled to put the key in the ignition. A panic was setting in. Finally he started the car and squealed out of his driveway.

●

The drive to Monika's was fast. As he pulled up in front of her place, James noted a similar scene as the one that morning at school. There was a small crowd milling around, behind yellow police tape. Some of the crowd were dressed in business clothes, some were in their dressing gowns and some were in casual attire. Two police cars were parked nearby. James parked his car as close as he could to Monika's place. He got out. He made his way through the crowd and up to the police line. There was a barricade to the front entrance of Monika's house and an officer standing guard. James tried to push his way by, in disregard to the officer's questions. The officer stopped him. There was a brief conversation. The officer let him pass after James mumbled something about,

"Girlfriend…"

James found his way through the open front doorway and into the hall of Monika's house. It was a mess. Everything was thrown all over the place. There were several policemen standing about, and others examining things. James became suddenly fearful that Monika might be hurt or…he wouldn't allow himself the thought.

He walked carefully down the hallway and to his right into the main living room. He caught sight of Monika seated on the sofa amidst the shambles of the room. She was safe. James felt an involuntary tinge of relief shoot through him. There were a couple of plainclothes policemen near her.

"Monika!?" he focused his gaze upon her as she looked up. "Are you okay?"

"Oh…James!" she stood up in joy at seeing his

arrival. She opened her arms to him.

James went forward to her. They embraced.

Monika felt the firm strength of his body as she hugged him. James felt her nervous trembling from the ordeal.

"Oh James…Thank you." she uttered before she became teary. She burrowed her face into his chest.

"There…There. Everything's okay." he replied as he squeezed harder. Her trembling was noticeably beginning to subside with the comfort of his warmth and strength. He felt a surge of anger at this violation of Monika's home, and yet was exhilarated by this intimacy with her.

Monika quietly wept. She felt the soft silk of James' shirt against her face. There was a sweet mustiness to it. Although she felt the taut strength of James the man she was now embraced with, it reminded her of her father. It was comforting and secure. She did not feel so alone and vulnerable. Coming to her senses, Monika suddenly realized that her tears had made James' shirt wet.

"Oh…I'm sorry. Your shirt." she pulled back as she spoke, drawing James' attention to the tears that had been absorbed by the silk.

"Oh…Don't be concerned. It's fine." he spoke softly. "I suppose now I will be under your spell."

he smiled and stared into her blue eyes.

Monika was puzzled for a moment, then understood the meaning of what James was really saying and returned his smile. For a second it seemed as if there was no one else present in the room, except James.

All of this encounter was being observed by a man who had been talking to Monika as James had arrived. James' attention was moved from Monika to this man as he broke from his embrace with her. The man was wearing a dark-ish out of fashion suit and was unkempt in his appearance. He was in his mid fifties. The man was staring directly at James with curiosity. With his left arm still around and consoling Monika, James offered his right hand to the man. The man reciprocated and moved towards him.

"Detective Atero." was all he verbally offered as he awaited a reply.

"James. James Anstey." He did not recall Atero from the school parking lot incident.

The brief introductions between the two men sobered Monika back from her fright.

"I'm...I'm sorry. Detective Atero?" Monika was sounding uncertain.

"Yes." Atero understood.

"James Anstey." Noticing that Atero wanted

more, she continued, "We work together."

"Hello, again." there was a suspicious air to Atero. This pulled both Monika's and James' attention away from each other, and more to an awareness of Atero and the activity and clutter within the room. Atero picked up on their sense of change.

"Quite a mess." Detective Atero was in control. James nodded in acknowledgment.

"Maybe we could all continue this over …ah…" Atero looked around and indicated the hallway that led to the kitchen. "…ahm…Over there?" He raised his right arm as he spoke, to suggest they go out of the living room and down the hall into the kitchen.

"Sure." James answered, though he was not aware of where the hall led. He assumed that there must be another room beyond that was more private.

Monika and James followed the Detective through the clutter, down the hall and into the small kitchen, which overlooked a now dark back garden.

The kitchen was very bright and decorated in the Spanish motif. Detective Atero proffered two chairs at a small round pedestalled breakfast table tucked closely against the wall on the other side of the sink and counter area. As Monika and James sat down, Detective Atero raised himself up onto the white marble countertop. James took the farthest seat away from but facing Atero; Monika was closest with her back just towards the Detective. She twisted the chair around to see him better.

Detective Atero was placing his right hand into his jacket breast pocket, and pulled out a crumpled package of non filtered cigarettes. He offered them to Monika, then James,

"Smoke?"

James replied first,

"No thanks."

"No, but go ahead. I don't mind." Monika encouraged.

"Well, if it's all right."

Atero struck the package against his left fist, and out popped a couple of slim virginal white paper wrapped cigarettes, each with loose brown tobacco extruding from their ends. He brought the package up to his face, and secured one of the cigarettes with his lips gradually removing it as he pulled the package away. While he was doing this, his left hand had gone to his left outside pocket, and was rummaging for something. A brass lighter was removed after a quick search, while his other hand returned the package to his inside pocket. Monika and James marveled at the perfect choreography of the movements. Each blended efficiently without direction and was perfectly timed together. Atero acknowledged their noticing of his ritual,

"Years of the bad habit."

He then brought the lighter up to the cigarette which was twitching between his lips, flipped back its lid, drew in a deep breath; focused his efforts on holding the cigarette still and into the burst of flame exuding from the lighter; then closing the lid to the lighter, leaving a smell of lighter fluid, and burning tobacco; placing the lighter back into his outside pocket; taking the cigarette between the first two fingers of his left hand, and exhaling through his nose and mouth as he spoke,

"I've been trying to stop for years." Smoke filled the room. "Only time I smoke, is when I'm on a job. The wife thinks I stopped two years ago." he chuckled, realizing that she probably knew that he still smoked, but not in her presence. It was a little game they played.

Monika and James smiled. They found Atero entertaining.

"Well," Atero abruptly changed back into the Detective. "Any idea who could have done this?"

Monika glanced towards James and then Atero, and shrugging said,

"N...n...no. I just moved to Los Angeles. I don't know who could do such a thing. I don't know anybody here yet. Just James."

"How did you know about this?" Detective Atero turned to James.

"A message on my answering machine. It was strange."

"Strange?" Atero pursued.

"Yeah. Did you or any of your men try to call me earlier?"

"No."

"There was a call, from a man. I didn't recognize the voice. I tried to pick up, but he hung up."

"What did he say?"

"Something about: 'Tell your ...girlfriend...she has what we want...Tell her...' and that's it. He hung up."

"And you didn't recognize the voice?"

"No."

"What is it that you have? Does this make any sense to you?" the Detective asked Monika.

"I don't know. It's crazy. First the car, then...Do you think there's a connection?"

"It's unlikely." Atero silently thought there might be but did not wish to alarm Monika.

"Wait a minute. There were footsteps. Footsteps, before yours."

"What do you mean? What do you remember?" Atero pushed calmly.

"Before you found me. There was someone else here in the house. Coming for me."

"Who was coming?"

"I don't know." Monika was flustered. She fell silent as she recalled the events before Detective Atero had 'rescued' her.

She recalled the darkness, the uncertainty. She was beginning to become fearful again as she now relived those moments. She saw the scene in her mind. She could feel the claustrophobic closet, with light glowing through under the door. The solid footsteps that had come into her room and then stopped. A voice calling out. Then a walking away. The voice was familiar, but she could not place it. The agony of not knowing. The waiting. The fear. A long silence. Then there were footsteps again. They were coming closer. They were different footsteps, and there seemed to be more of them. Then there were voices. The footsteps came closer. Closer, and closer. They were coming right to her. Someone grabbed the handle of the closet door. She watched as it turned. As the door began to open, she pushed herself deeper into the back of the closet. She couldn't hold it any longer. She had screamed…

"Monika. Monika are you all right?" James tried to break through.

"Miss. Queller? It's okay. You're safe." Atero added, noticing her trance-like state, and understanding what was going through her mind.

"I was so frightened. I didn't know what would happen to…" Monika brought her left hand to her mouth as she broke from her trance.

"Detective Atero. Couldn't we continue this tomorrow?" James was not asking. They had each been through a lot today, and a break was needed.

Realizing that he wouldn't get much else from Monika, Detective Atero agreed.

"Yes. That's fine. First thing tomorrow. At the station. Okay?" He took out a card and placed it on the table between them. "10:30?"

Detective Atero got off the countertop, and stood back up in the kitchen,

"Is there someplace you could stay this evening, other than here? Family?" he directed this to Monika through James.

"Yes. She can stay with me, at my place."

Monika was about to protest, but realized that she would rather not be left alone. She trusted James.

"Thank you." was all she said.

"Good. I'm sure everything will be fine, but just to be on the safe side…It would be better for you to be with someone…away from here." Atero was being diplomatic.

"I know. I'd rather not be alone right now anyway." Monika agreed.

As they spoke, one of the other plainclothes officers came into the kitchen looking for Detective Atero.

"Detective? We're all through here now."

"Okay Mark. Thanks. You guys go ahead. I'll be a few more moments.

"Okay. See you back at the station." The plainclothes officer turned, and on his way out of the house, gathered the remaining policemen.

"I'll see you tomorrow." Atero said to the officer and then turned back to his interrogees,

"If there is anything else you remember, or if anything else happens, please call."

Atero then said his good-nights, and left the kitchen walking down the hall and out through the front door, which he closed after him.

James was now standing. He moved over to Monika. They were alone.

"Come on. Get your jacket. Let's go. We need to get away from here."

Monika looked up as she stood,

"Thank you, James." was all she said.

They walked down the hall and as they went James turned off the house lights at the main switch. Monika took a jacket from the rack adjacent to the front entry. James opened the door. Before she left, Monika remembered her father's old briefcase. It was still sitting on the floor where she had earlier placed it. She picked it up by its old leather handle, turned, and walked out. James followed, making sure that the door was secure after it was closed. He would come over to repair it tomorrow.

As they walked down the pathway that led towards James' parked car, about one hundred feet to the left parked in the dark, was a late model sedan. Other eyes were watching. From inside this car, Monika's house could easily be surveyed. From the sedan, a clear view of the path that Monika and James now took was visible. A dark male figure was sitting behind the driver's side. He saw them get into the red sports car. He was answering questions on a cellular phone as he watched.

"No."

".............."

"There wasn't anything."

"............"

"No."

"..................................."

"Didn't find it."

"............"

"No."

"...................."

"They're leaving now."

"..."

"The girl and the boyfriend."

"...

....

..............."

"Yeah."

"...................................."

"Yeah."

"...

................."

"Okay." he ended the call.

Flipping the phone closed, he placed it back on the bench seat to his right. He waited as the red Corvette started, turned on its lights, signaled and pulled out into the quiet street. He then started his car, and after the Corvette was under way, turned on his headlights and slowly pulled after them. He kept his eye on the Corvette's tail lights. He was under orders and did not want to lose them, but he did not want them to know that he was following.

●

The trip to James' would not take long. Both he and Monika sat in silence. Monika was far away in thought, and James did not want to force her back to reality by breaking the silence with inane conversation. After a while Monika spoke,

"What do they want?"

"They?"

Their silence was broken. Monika was tired, frustrated and still panicked over the past, as well as the most recent, strange events.

"Who did this? Why me? What are they after?"

James shrugged in reply. He kept both his hands on the steering wheel as he continued the drive. He realized that Monika was thinking out loud, more than expecting an answer from him. She was not speaking to him, but for the benefit of her own piece of mind.

"What do they want? What is the reason?" she searched her memory of the past few days, looking for a common thread that linked these events together. Something that might give a clue as to who was responsible and what they wanted from her. The vandalism to her car; the terror at her home; the phone calls; these images all ran through her thoughts.

"We want it." Monika repeated out loud.

"What?" James was not sure if she was asking him for something.

"The calls at work. What is it that they want? What are they looking for?" as she spoke, she began a visual search. "My briefcase. Where is it?"

"Don't worry. It's there. Behind your seat. There…" James attempted to point while driving. "There. In the back."

As she twisted her upper body Monika undid her seat belt in order to get visual confirmation that the briefcase was behind her. There it was, squeezed behind her seat. She leaned towards it and half rising, fumbled at, then managed to grab, its handle. She lifted and brought it out, placing it upon her lap as she twisted and sat back firmly in her seat. She scrutinized it. A thought came to her,

"The briefcase. That's it! My father's briefcase. It's something…something about the briefcase."

As Monika spoke, James made a hard turn. Not far behind, the headlights of another car copied his maneuver. James did not notice.

"It has to be."

"I don't get it. It's just an old briefcase."

"My father…he worked for the government. It was something secret. He didn't tell me about it.

Before…he died, I remember there were calls. I remember after one call, seeing a look on his face. It was a look of fear." she paused. "Then they were gone."

She drifted into the memory of the loss of her parents. It had been after their traditional Sunday luncheon. She had arrived late, and had come alone, William had had some last minute work to do. They had argued. She was upset with William. She had wondered if it was worth having a boyfriend, who was always disappearing at the last moment on important work. She had asked him what he wanted from their relationship. She wanted more of a commitment. He did not. As a result, they had decided to break up. Monika was angry, but when she arrived at her parents' home, she had resolved not to let her disappointment with William ruin the day with her parents.

She remembered how that day had been beautiful and clear. The sound of the ocean was rolling upon the sandy beach just a few yards away from the cedar deck that they were all seated upon. The lunch was set and they were all casually chatting and eating. It was idyllic.

She heard the ring of the portable phone and her father answering. He had moved off to one side and it was obvious to her and her mother that there was something wrong. Her father's voice was guarded and sounded panicked. There was an argument...and then he hung up without completing his conversation. He was agitated and gave a strange look to her mother. She asked what *'that'* had been all about. He had replied as casually as he could, nothing, just more problems at the office. He then had resumed lunch as if nothing had happened. Nothing more was said. Monika had felt concerned for her father, but had said nothing. She had felt the whole phone conversation odd and that her father was not being truthful with her, but had not pursued her suspicions.

After they had finished eating, they had spent the rest of that afternoon together there without further interruption. Though they tried to conceal it, there had been a change in her parents' mood. Around 6:00 PM Monika decided to quickly go to the corner store and get some cigarettes and some exercise after eating all of the fabulous food.

"See you in a minute." she recalled her last words said to them. How she wished she had known that these were to be the last ones.

Upon her return some twenty minutes later. Her life was abruptly changed. The front door of the house was open. She had thought that perhaps she had not closed it properly, but then noticed as she entered that the house was in chaos. She panicked and feared for the worst. She had called out to her parents but there had been no response. She had run to the deck. The whole place was a mess. The table was overturned and plates and food scattered everywhere. Her parents were not to be found. She recalled the pain of the realization that something may have happened to them...

"Monika." James' voice broke her from her recall. "What is it?"

"This is so odd. My father worked for the Government. There's something wrong. Something about the briefcase."

She unclasped the briefcase, opened it and began to rifle through it. There were all of her papers, files etcetera. She pulled them from the case and threw them on the floor of the car. When it was finally emptied, she turned the briefcase upside down and shook it, but nothing other than dust and dirt fell out.

"There has to be something. Something."

She put the briefcase back upon her lap and began to probe its insides with her fingertips. The inside was lined with a smooth red leather. She scrutinized the interior. There was a tear on one side and a piece of paper protruding from between the lining that she had never noticed before. She tried to pull it, but there was not enough of a tear to get it out. She tore at the lining and was then able to remove the paper. It was an envelop. James was intrigued as he tried to watch and drive at the same time.

"Pull over. Now."

James looked left and right, checked his rear view mirror, and pulled over without signaling, coming to a quick stop at the side of the road.

Not far behind another car copied these actions, remaining a hundred or so feet behind, just beyond their view.

As they came to a stop, Monika had ripped open the envelop and removed what appeared to be a one page letter from inside it. She began to read.

"What's it say?"

"It's from my father,"

> *"…If something happens to me, go to the University… Go to the University Post Office…"*

she repeated,

> *"…and ask for the contents of '1021'. Be very careful. Be certain you are not followed."*

"What?"

"There's a phone number: 415 555 1692. That's the Bay area."

The note had been obviously written in haste. Monika recognized the familiar blue ink of her father's fountain pen. She drew the letter to her bosom, closed her eyes, and drew in a short breath. She then looked up and over to James. Her eyes met his,

"I don't understand."

James did not reply. He was also at a loss.

"We have to go to Palo Alto."

"Palo Alto?"

"Yes. Stanford. My father was doing research there. At SLAC."

"S L A C?"

"Stanford Linear Accelerator. He was working on something secret for the Government. It involved the accelerator. I don't know what, but we have to go there. To the Post Office. Box 1021. That's what's behind all of this." It was all beginning to make sense to her now, "Whoever 'they' are, they're after this letter, and whatever's in Box 1021. That's why they broke into my car and apartment."

Monika became suddenly silent as she began to fully understand the scope of what was going on and that she had unwittingly exposed James to a possible treacherous situation. She became more concerned, "I think we are both in danger. Now they're after you too. I'm really sorry. I didn't know."

"That explains the message on my machine." James seemed unperturbed.

"Message?" Monika had forgotten about the message that James had mentioned to Atero.

"Yeah. The one I got at home. It was a man's voice. It said it knew my girlfriend had what they wanted."

"Oh yeah that's right." Monika remembered. It was all becoming clear to her. "We can't go to your place. They're probably there, waiting. We have to go now, as we are."

"Are you sure?"

"Yes. I don't want you to get hurt. We can't take the chance. They know who you are and where you live. Our only chance is to get to Palo Alto, before they can know where we are going."

"What about that number? Maybe we should call it?"

"Yes. Whoever it is, they must be able to help. My father must have trusted them or he wouldn't have given the number."

"Okay. It's about a five hour drive. We can call the number on the way up."

Their panic was now replaced with paranoia.
They felt as if they were being watched. James
signaled, and looked in his side mirror as he
pulled back onto the road. A flash of a set of headlights caught his eye as he came onto the road.
Monika sensed James' mood.

"What is it?"

"I think we're being followed already. Don't
look back."

Monika's heart raced.

"I'll turn here and see."

James turned and after a few moments the headlights reappeared in his rear view mirror.

"They're there again."

Monika stole a quick look and saw the two
headlights behind. James picked up speed and so
did the headlights behind them. They stayed with
them. He turned again. The lights reappeared.

"Hold on I'm going to try and lose them."

James put his foot to the floor. Within seconds
the car behind, obviously realizing that it had
been detected, picked up speed. The chase was
on. The streets were not busy as it was now late.
The two cars rushed down the road. There was a
periodic squealing of tires as James' speed
became very fast. They drove very dangerously as
they raced through the city streets. They turned

several times and ran a couple of red lights. The car behind stuck to them. In fact, it was beginning to gain on them.

"Are they still there?"

"Yes. They're behind. I can see them. They're gaining on us. We'll have to lose them before we get on the freeway."

With that said James made a very hard turn, and went down an alley. It was tight. His nerves were taut as he sped along it. The other car followed. If anyone was to suddenly jump out from any crevice in the ally, there would be no chance of stopping. James hoped that would not happen. Monika tensed in anticipation.

"Look out!" she yelled.

A small pair of eyes reflected in James' lights. James swerved and made another hard turn along an adjoining alley way. This alley was full of garbage cans and debris. The debris flew over and around James car after being hit. The car behind was still in pursuit, but had slowed. James sped up. Up ahead was the main road. He drove through some cardboard boxes and turned onto the main road. The boxes flew overhead and emptied all sorts of paper into the air in the alley. It obscured the view. The car behind had no choice but to slow down. In these few seconds James had made it to the main road, and sped along.

"Are they still there?"

James made a turn onto another road, and waited a few moments before answering,

"No. We seem to have lost them."

They drove on towards the freeway and Palo
Alto. They felt safe for the moment.

●

Behind in the alley the other car had stopped. A
pair of hands pulled out a small calculator-like
devise from the glove compartment. The devise
was opened to reveal a small screen which was
flashing and indicating something. It was a hom-
ing devise. The hands placed the devise on the
seat, and returned to the steering wheel. Slowly
the car moved on and out of the alley. It made the
same turn at the roadway that James had made.
The driver of this car was still in pursuit. He
would continue to follow and make his move at a
different time and place.

Chapter 4

Monika and James were now well on their way to Palo Alto. James had been driving for over four hours. It had been a very smooth drive. Not many other cars were on the freeway, and in the darkness the miles had gone by quickly. It was now in the early morning hours. Both he and Monika were exhausted. They hadn't seen anyone following them and they were confident that they had lost their tail. James had been the only one driving since they started the trip. He needed to stop for a break. He turned on the car's right signal.

"Low on gas?" Monika questioned. She had been half asleep, but the sudden clicking sound of the signal roused her.

"Yes. But I think we should stop here for some rest. I'm beat." As he spoke, James caressed her hand.

Monika responded with a smile. She did not object to James' suggestion. She was tired and wanted to lie in a comfortable bed. The seat was awkward and she was not able to get a restful sleep. She welcomed the stop. There was still plenty of time to get to Palo Alto.

They pulled off the freeway and into a gas station. It was a small station in the middle of nowhere. James pulled up to the gas pumps and stopped the car. The station was not busy. He yawned and stretched. It felt good to be in relative silence away from the freeway and the noise of his car engine. He opened his door and noticed how silent the area was. It was so peaceful here. He got out of the car and went to the pump. Choosing premium grade, he took the nozzle and turned on the pump. It immediately zeroed and primed itself. James unscrewed the gas cap, put the nozzle in and began to fill up his tank with fuel.

By now Monika had also gotten out and was

stretching her legs. They were the only ones there filling up. The only noise was coming from the freeway.

"I'm going to make that call."

"Okay."

Monika walked over to a phone booth at the far side of the gas station. She had the letter from the briefcase in her hand. The phone booth was not well cared for. She entered into it through its broken folding door. After picking up the receiver, she pulled out a credit card from her purse and placing it in the slot in the phone, swiped it across the card reader. The screen paused a moment as it validated her card, then displayed 'thank you'. Monika heard a dial tone. She dialed the number. It rang three times. Then,

"Leave your name, and phone number."

It was an abrupt computer voice. Monika was startled.

"Beep."

"My name is Monika Queller, I found this number." as she spoke, unbeknownst to her, the call was being identified. "I'll have to call again. I don't have a phone where you can call me. I need some help."

She hung up the phone and turned to go back to the car. Far away and within seconds the phone booth number was displayed and tagged to her message by the computer answering devise. It would be forwarded immediately.

James had finished his fill up and returned from paying the attendant as Monika returned.

"Any luck?'

"No. It must be too late. I left a message that I would try again."

"The attendant says there's a nice little motel just up the road."

"Sounds fine."

They got back into the car and drove off. They drove up the service road that ran parallel to the freeway. It was a quaint area. After about two miles they came to a motel. It was old and a red neon light blurted out its name into the night: Aloha Motel. Its architecture was in the Spanish motif. It was very run down. Its driveway was crumbling and had many pot holes. The place had seen better days. James turned and drove carefully up the driveway. He pulled up in front of the office and shut off the car.

"I'll go in. Okay?" James said as he opened his door and got out.

It suddenly seemed cool outside. James adjusted his jacket and went into the office to register. Monika waited in the car. She surveyed the area as best she could by the glow of the old neon sign. Her thoughts changed for a moment. There was probably only one bed in the room. She felt nervous, tired and elated.

James opened the office door and stepped into an area that only had room for a counter and a chair. It was very cramped. The office was dirty which suggested to him that the whole motel was probably not clean, but James did not care. He just wanted a place to sleep. He was greeted by a fat balding man who was in his bedclothes and seated behind the counter.

"Good evening. Just the night?" James was asked.

"Yes."

The man peered through the office window and saw Monika in the car and smiled,

"Two?"

"Yes."

"I've only got double beds."

"That'll be fine."

The man filled out a form and passed it to James to sign,

"$31.89. How are you paying?"

"Cash." James took out his wallet and gave the man two twenties.

The man gave him change and the key,

"It's right next to the pop machine."

"Thanks." James took the change and the key and left.

The man watched as James exited and walked back to his car. James opened the car door and got back into his seat. He said:

"Number 6."

Monika did not respond. She was a little nervous.

He started the car and backed out a short distance to enable himself to turn and move on forward. He then drove about fifty feet and parked in front of the pop machine and Number 6.

"Here we are."

He smiled at her as he turned the car off and pulled the keys out of the ignition. She smiled back.

They both got out of the car. Monika followed as James went to the door and put the key in the handle and opened it. The room was dark inside. James felt for the light switch. He found it just inside to the left of the door frame. He turned it on. Instantly the yellow glow of old lights revealed the interior of the place.

The room was small and dreary. It needed a good coat of paint. There was a television on an old rickety stand, one large bed with a dingy red covering, two bedside tables and wall lamps which were controlled by the main light switch, a stained green carpet, an old yellow Princess phone, and the door that led to the bathroom. The curtains were drawn which kept out peering eyes and the bright lights from the front, but not the neon red glow of the motel sign.

"It ain't the St. Francis, but it will do." Monika was first to speak as she stood reluctant to enter, but forced herself into the room. She was too tired to care about the condition of the quarters.

"It's only for a few hours." James walked over to check out the bathroom, as Monika plunked herself onto the bed.

"Which side do you want?" Monika realized that it would not be fair to make James sleep on the floor after all they had now been through.

"The one closest to the door. Do you want to…?" James nonchalantly replied, and indicated the use of the bathroom.

"No. Go ahead." she found his shyness attractive. "I'll wait."

James shrugged acknowledgment and closed the door after him as he entered the small bathroom. Once the door was closed both of them separately gave out a nervous sigh.

Several quiet moments passed. Monika could

now hear the water of the running shower. It soothed her. Sitting on the bed, she began to remove her clothing. As she unbuttoned her top, her thoughts lingered and became mesmerized by the sound of James in the shower…

…It had been a long drive. James was worn. He needed to take a warm shower. He turned on the water, which at first was cool and rusty in color, then became more clear and hot. He adjusted the temperature. He then pulled off his clothes, dropping them to the floor, and stepped over them and into the shower's caress. It felt good. He put his head into the water and lost himself in the pleasure of the sensation. He pushed his fingers through his hair forcing the water over and running down his muscular back.

James was so totally immersed in the feel and sound of the water, that he did not notice the brass colored bathroom door handle as it slowly turned and unlocked. He did not hear the door as it was pried more and more open. He did not see the person who then walked into the room towards the shower. Suddenly without warning, the opaque shower door was opened. James was caught off guard,

"Wha…?!" he called out as he wiped the water from his face so that he could identify the intruder.

It was Monika. James' fear turned quickly to desire. His heart missed a beat. She was beautiful. He felt a wave of emotion surge up within him as Monika's eyes slowly lifted up, caressing his features till finally they met his welcoming gaze. Her hair was long. He had not noticed how long before. She brushed it back and revealed her supple breasts. She stepped into the water and into his arms. They embraced. She felt his warmth through their wetness. She felt his firm body pushing against hers. She leaned back into the shower, still in his embrace. The water massaged her face and ran down her skin. He bowed his head to her inviting bosom and kissed in passionate excitement. She accepted his desire and sighed as if under the power of a potent drug.

They were in their own world of sensual delight and anticipation. The sound of the water cocooning them from the real world. They kissed. She felt his hard body pressing more frantically against her soft skin. Monika broke from the kiss, and turned off the water with one free hand. She gave him a lustful stare and then kissed him, her lips were soft and moist. James lifted her firmly into his arms and opening the shower door, carried her from the shower and bathroom into the main room and to the bed. Gently he placed her upon it. Not a word was spoken. She shivered but not from the cold. She wanted him, and he wanted her. She raised her arms to him, inviting him. He fell into her embrace.

●

At the Gas station down the road from the motel a dark car pulled up. It was early in the pre-dawn morning. A thin blond haired man wearing cowboy boots got out and walked over to the attendant in the kiosk. He did not want gasoline.

"Good Morning, sir."

"Morning."

"What can I get you?"

"Have you seen this woman?"

He offered a small photograph. The attendant took it. He recognized the picture, but did not let on. He did not want to get involved.

"No can't say I have."

"Well thanks anyway." The man did not believe him. His tone was of displeasure. The attendant understood and tried to extricate himself from what he sensed might be a potentially dangerous situation.

"But I only just came on shift. You'd be better asking Sana. He works the nights."

"Where is this Sana?"

"Out back, getting ready to leave."

"Thanks." The man was satisfied and hurried out to find Sana. He went around the back of the kiosk and saw a younger man getting on a motorbike and preparing to start it up.

"Hi. The guy inside said you work the nights?" the blond spoke loudly.

"Yeah. Just leaving."

"Can you tell me if you've seen this woman?" he offered the picture as he approached the motorbike. Sana took the photo from him.

"Well sure. She was here with a man a few hours ago. She didn't come in but her man did. Filled up and wanted to know if there was any place to spend the night."

"Is there?"

"Up the road about two miles."

"Did you see if they went that way?"

"Yeah. They went." Sana gave the photo back. "Are they murderers or something?"

"No." the blond thought quickly, "I'm a P.I. She's run off from her husband, and he's hired me to find her."

"Well I'll be. If that don't beat all. Women. Well, I hope you find that bitch." Sana laughed as he got on his bike and started it.

"Thanks alot." shouted the blond man over the

noise of the motor. He waved as Sana pulled away.

The man put the picture back into his jacket pocket and crossed over to the phone booth. He entered the booth and checked the phone number, then smiled. It was the correct number. He exited the booth and took a long look up the road. It was early light. Still smiling, he returned to his car, got in and started the engine. Slowly he pulled off and drove up the road to the Aloha Motel.

●

James was asleep. Monika lay in his arms awake. They were both warm beneath the covers. The dawn was beginning to break. It was a moment of carefree serenity. Monika had a glow about her. She was examining him with her eyes. She was happy to have been with him. She leaned over and kissed him on the cheek. Gradually he awoke.

"Good morning." she beamed.

"Oh…So it wasn't a dream."

"No. Do you wish it was?"

"Yes."

"Why?" Monika was offended by his response. James grinned,

"Cause then it would be like last night forever."

She climbed over top him and felt the warmth of

his body between her thighs. She bent down and kissed him. They began to make love.

●

A dark car slowly pulled up to the motel office.

●

"What time is it?"

Monika turned to see her watch which was on the bedside table. With her movement the bed sheet fell. James watched. He viewed her delicate skin, curving from her thighs to the outline of her breasts, with desire. She was voluptuous.

"6:30." she announced as she turned back to him. She caught the glint in his eyes, and understood.

"Now what were you looking at?" she was playful.

James grabbed her and pulled her onto him.

"I'll give you one guess."

The words were left hanging as a loud pounding came at their door.

Monika and James became silent. A chill of terror ran through them. They were jerked out of their dream world and back to the reality of their situation. They looked to each other. They each instantly suspected that it was their pursuer. James put his index finger to his lips to indicate silence. He whispered,

"I'll answer the door. If it's the maid I'll send her away. If anything else happens, you hit them from behind." He indicated that she should get up and go to behind the door.

"Okay." she whispered in understanding.

Monika quietly got up from the bed and wrapped the bedsheet around her nakedness. She climbed over the bed and crossed the room to behind where the front door would be, when it opened. She took one of the heavy bedside lamps with her. She waited, holding the lamp in two hands above her head while also trying to keep the sheet around her.

James called out as he rose from the bed and quickly pulled on his underwear,

"Who is it?"

There was no answer just more knocking.

"Alright give me a second." He picked up his trousers and put then on.

James made his way to the door. There was no peep hole. He carefully moved the curtains and peered through. On the outside standing in front of the door was a tough looking man. James turned his view to Monika. He indicated to her to be ready as he continued to mutter.

"Okay. I hear you. Hang on."

As James unlocked the door it was pushed open,

and the man came through. Everything happened so fast. Before she knew what she was doing, Monika, with eyes closed, brought the lamp down upon the man's head. This knocked him unconscious and to the floor before he could say a word, or knew what was happening to him. The man fell face first to the floor. James bent down next to the unconscious man and turned him over in order to see who it was. Monika gasped,

"William!?"

"You know this guy?"

"It's my ex-boyfriend."

"Boyfriend? What's he doing here?"

"I don't know, and I don't trust him."

"Get dressed. Quickly. I'm not waiting to find out. Maybe he's one of 'them'."

James got up and closed the door. There was no time to waste. The man would soon regain consciousness.

"Get dressed. We've got to get out of here." he directed Monika.

They both threw on their clothing and gathered their belongings. William was still lying unconscious upon the floor. Within seconds Monika and James were both stepping over him and out of the room. They hurriedly crossed over and got into the car. James started it. He roughly put the car into gear. The wheels squealed as he backed up and away from the motel.

As they were driving off William started to come around. He picked himself up and still a little dazed, ran out of the door. He shouted after them to stop. It was too late. He was not heard as they sped down the road and back towards the freeway. William ran to his own car in order to chase after them. He searched for his keys enroute to his car, but soon realized that he did not have them. He must have dropped them after he was knocked out. He stood looking after James and Monika as they escaped. Frustrated by the situation, he threw his arms angrily to his side. A cloud of dust was billowing from James' car as it speedily traveled down the road. Soon the car was out of sight. It was getting away. There was nothing that William could do.

James was relieved that they were not being followed by Monika's ex-boyfriend. He was a little aggravated that an obviously jealous boyfriend had been stalking them without their knowledge. As Monika and James pulled onto the freeway another car picked up their tail. It was not William. In all the excitement, it went unnoticed.

"How did he know you were there?" James was short with Monika.

"I don't know."

"Nobody knew where we were. No-one was following. I don't get it."

"The call." Monika put it together.

"Call?"

"The one I made from the gas station. It must have been traced."

"So you think your 'X' is involved?"

"I don't know. But how would he have known how to find me. He must somehow be connected."

"Yeah, but is he a good guy or a bad guy?"

"I don't know. If he found us as a result of my call, he might be a good guy."

"Maybe, and maybe not. He sure wasn't acting like one. You'd better not call that number again till after we've got whatever is in that box in Palo Alto."

"Yeah. But why would my father have written down that number?"

James did not respond.

●

Behind them on the freeway, from within the following car, there was a steady strong beep. The signal was homed in on James' vehicle. The driver took out a compact folded phone from his jacket inside pocket, opened it, and pressed one of its buttons causing the phone to automatically dial a number.

"I've ah…found them."

"……………………………"

"Yeah."

"…………"

"Yeah."

"………………………………………………………………………………………………………"

"I'll follow him all the way."

"…………"

"Yeah."

"…………"

"On the way to San Francisco."

"………………………………………………………………"

"No problem."

The man folded the phone to end the conversation, and placed it back in his chest pocket. During the conversation, he had kept his eyes fixed upon James' car which was about two hundred feet ahead. He did not want to risk losing sight of them no matter how remote the possibility of that happening. He kept a safe distance behind. Both of the cars moved quickly up the freeway.

●

At the Aloha Motel, William, still unable to

find his keys, was now standing inside the office and using the phone. He dialed a 415 exchange. A computer voice mail system answered:

"Leave your name, and phone number."

"They're on their way." was all that William said. He then hung up the phone. He was still upset at losing them. He should have anticipated their reaction.

The motel office appeared even more dirty and small in the morning light. The balding fat man in his sixties was sitting near the counter nervously pretending to do some paperwork. He was the manager. The stale smell of his half smoked unlit cigar filled the space. William spoke to him,

"Thanks."

The manager nodded and grunted around the cigar in acknowledgment. William turned and left the office in search of his keys. Once found, he would then go and travel north after Monika and James.

●

The computer voice mail machine dialed automatically. High up in the center of San Francisco within the TransAmerica Pyramid, in a plush office, a modern design phone upon a glass table, rang. It was answered by a well dressed official looking man in his forties.

"Message forwarding. Please enter the code." it was the computer voice mail.

Upon recognizing the source of the call, he entered the code from the phone keypad.

"Thank you." was responded by the machine, followed by a brief pause, and then,

"There is one message,"

There was another short pause and then the play back of the digitally recorded message,

"They're on their way."

The man hung up the phone and smiled. After a moment of thought, he again picked up the phone and dialed. After three rings there was an answer. He spoke in a flat tone,

"They're on their way. Get your people rolling." That was it.

He hung up the phone, and turned to look out of the office window upon the misty skyline of the Golden Gate Bridge and Alcatraz. The early morning mist was still heavy. It blanketed the Bay area like soft billowing pure white cotton. It stretched from inside the bay over and past the Golden Gate and on to the horizon. Only the towering red suspension supports and wires of the bridge could be seen as they pierced through the 'cotton puff'.

"It won't be much longer now." he said out loud

to himself as he drew in this panoramic marvel.

●

The last leg of their drive up the freeway was almost complete. The trouble at the motel was far behind them. Neither Monika nor James seemed overly concerned or aware that they might still be being followed. It was a typically beautiful Bay Area day. The sky was azure blue and the sun was becoming warmer and warmer as the morning progressed.

When they came to the outskirts of San José the traffic became heavier. It was the beginning of the weekend rush hour. They had plenty of time and were now only a half an hour away from the university. The Post Office at Stanford would be open till noon.

Monika knew this area well, having spent many years here. She began to tell James the necessary directions.

"Just stay on 101 going to Palo Alto. When we get closer, there will be a couple of signs. Get off at Palm Drive."

"Okay." James acknowledged as he concentrated on the traffic.

James stayed in the express lanes as they sped through San José.

When they had passed through San José,

Monika spoke out,

"We're almost there." she sounded a little concerned. James picked up the serious tone in her voice.

"Don't worry. It'll be fine." James comforted as they drove on to their destination.

They both now realized that they were approaching the next level of their journey. They hadn't really considered before what might await them there. They had been so busy escaping from whatever danger was pursuing them that their minds had not spent any time on such thoughts. Now, for the first time they thought about their immediate future and the possible dangers ahead. They fell into a tense silence.

Absorbed by these new fears they drove on and it was not long before they found themselves entering into the greater university area. The sights began to get very familiar to Monika. It would not be much further before they would be at the exit to the university. Several exits came and went. Monika expected that the next one would be theirs. She sat upright and kept her sight on the road signs. The sign for the exit came into view.

"There." Monika pointed to the sign, "Turn off here."

James signaled and changed lanes to get to the off ramp. He slowed as he exited the freeway. The off ramp consisted of a sharp circular curve which brought them around to a bridge which passed over the freeway and went west to Palm Drive. From here they immediately entered onto the university campus after going past two large stone boundary markers.

Palm Drive ran as far as the eye could see. At its farthest end were the main buildings of the university, and behind them the foothills which rose up to the sky. The buildings were about a mile away from this entrance. The view was incredible. There was a long boulevard separating east from west lanes of Palm Drive. There were palm trees as well as eucalyptus trees; their pungent aroma lining Palm Drive along both sides and along the boulevard.

As they made their way up the road and came closer to the buildings, they could soon see the beautiful mosaic on the central most building ahead of them. This was the Stanford Chapel which towered over the other buildings in the Main Quadrangle. It evoked an emotion that Monika understood well. This was home. Not only had she grown up in the area, and visited her father at his work on campus, but also she had studied here. It was a piece of paradise on earth. There was a tranquillity here. A beauty that was inspiring.

"Wow." James took in the sight.

"Yeah. It's beautiful. Isn't it?"

There was a pause in their conversation as they continued up Palm Drive and took in the sight. The majesty of the sandstone buildings and how they blended in so perfectly with the natural environment was breathtaking. After several moments of silence, Monika continued with her directions,

"When we get there." she pointed out a large oval area in front of the buildings that the road went around, "At the far end. Park as close as you can in front. We will walk from there. It isn't far."

James followed her directions and continued up Palm Drive. Gradually the road curved more to the north and skirted the large grassy oval. It was well kept and green. Water was being pulsed by automatic sprinklers out fifty feet in semi circular repeated patterns over the grass of 'the Oval'. There were several volleyball nets set up on the Oval, but no-one was playing. A dirt path crossed through the middle of the Oval running past these nets which allowed pedestrians to walk through and on to the buildings of the Main Quadrangle.

They drove on to the top of the road where it

met the Main Quadrangle and the western most point of the Oval; then continued on along the side of the Oval and the Main Quadrangle. They drove south, parallel to their entry from the freeway. Being Saturday and still early, there were not many cars or people around. James pulled the car into a parking space in front of the buildings next to a large centrally placed archway through which could be seen the brilliant mosaic of the chapel.

"Now what?" he had stopped the car and looked inquisitively to Monika.

Monika noticed the time on the clock radio. It was now nine o'clock. The Post Office would not open till 9:30.

"We've got about half an hour. How about a coffee?"

Monika was rejuvenated by being back on the campus. It made her very nostalgic of that earlier time of her life when she lived here. A time of happiness without the harsh realities of the outside world. She appreciated this and was grateful to have had those times. She was elated to be back here and to have these feelings, regardless of the circumstances that had brought her back. She was glowing.

"Sure. That sounds great." James removed the keys from the ignition and prepared to open his door.

At the same time they both opened their doors and got out. James came round to Monika and took her hand. He kissed her gently on the cheek. They began to walk. Monika took the lead. They walked along the sidewalk and then up the steps through the arched entry and onto the Main Quadrangle. They were surrounded by the university's romantic Spanish sandstone structures of old California. The delicate fragrance of palm and eucalyptus trees filled the warm still air. The bougainvilleas were in brilliant pink and mauve blossom. It was an idyllic, inviting setting.

Monika was happy that she was sharing what she regarded as an intimacy with James. She felt light and happy. She began a brief tour guide routine. It was a spontaneous replay from her past. She used to volunteer as a tour guide on Saturdays while attending the university.

"This is the Main Quadrangle. That's Memorial Church, part of it was destroyed in the 1906 earthquake. It was rebuilt but the original roof design was never fully restored." she spoke as they crossed over the large open space in front of the church and came to the covered arched walkway of the History wing of the Quad. Under their feet was a marble sidewalk that went perimetrically around the Main Quadrangle. In every section of the sidewalk there were brass plaques centrally placed. It was like Hollywood, except the brass plaques were square and had two digits on them, rather than stars.

"Time capsules. Those are the class dates." Monika answered James' unasked question. "They start there," she indicated the spot by turning and pointing. "In 1891, and go once a year till now."

"Oh." James acknowledged. At the same time he was struck by this tradition he noted that this place felt more like an old time California ranch or farm, than an institution.

They continued on. In minutes they had passed through the Quad with its arched wings and marble sidewalks, onto a wide paved area and were passing other buildings not attached to the Main Quad. There were trees and plants everywhere. They eventually came to the main square and another row of buildings.

"That's the bookstore, and White Square. Over there is the Post Office. Around there is Tresidder Union. We can get coffee and stuff there."

"Okay." James was awed by both the sereneness and the beauty of the place. The sound of a fountain near the bookstore was soothing.

They walked on past these buildings and veered to the right to a larger complex that housed a large terrace. There were numerous black wire tables and chairs laid out. An occasional cyclist passed by Monika and James as they came closer to the terrace. A few people were scattered about the terrace sitting drinking coffee. Some were alone reading and others were chatting with friends and colleagues.

They walked up on to the terrace and went into a cafeteria style coffee shop. Monika got a coffee and a donut, James just a coffee. After paying they went back out and found an empty table from which they could view the Post Office across the way about one hundred feet. As they sat, more and more people steadily filled the area.

Over at the Post Office there were several people who looked like students, standing about, waiting for it to open for business. Everyone was relaxed and in casual dress, except for two men standing to the east side of the building wearing dark suits. They stood out on this warm sunny morning in such clothing. They were obviously outsiders, probably official visitors of some sort.

"So how long were you here?"

"Four years. I did my degree, but I grew up around here because of my father's job. So I've lived in the area for about ten years."

"It must have been wonderful."

"Yeah," Monika became distracted as she noted the two suited men by the Post Office.

"What's wrong?"

"Those men. Don' t they seem a little strange?" James scrutinized them,

"Maybe they're on business."

As if on cue the two men walked off and away from the Post Office. Gradually they went out of sight around the back of the Post Office building.

"See. They're gone. I think we're just a little sensitive."

"Yeah, maybe. But we should be careful. Maybe we were followed and we didn't know it?"

"No. I didn't see anybody."

"I hope you're right. I'm getting a little scared."

"Me too. But it will be fine. We'll go over when they open and get whatever's in that box. If we see those men come back we'll hang around here till they go."

"Okay. But after we get whatever's there, let's get right back to the car and out of here. Look," Monika observed. "It's opening a little earlier today."

"Speaking of that, how will you get the clerk to give you whatever's in box 1021? Won't he ask for I.D.?"

In all the excitement Monika had not considered the problem of getting access to the Post Office box. She thought for a moment. Then answered James' question,

"I'll say I've misplaced my key. Maybe that will work?"

"I hope so." James was not sure.

"I've done it before, when I was a student here. They are used to the occasional person asking. If we are lucky, the clerk will be the only one on and busy and not bother to ask for any identification. If I'm asked, I'll try and wing it." though nervous Monika appeared confident.

They finished their coffees and got up from their seats. The Post Office was just opening. The two men were nowhere to be seen.

"Well, here goes. Let's be careful. Keep an eye out for anything unusual."

They left the terrace and walked towards the Post Office. By the time they got there, it was completely open and a line of people waiting to be served had formed. Only one clerk was on duty. It was a typical Saturday. Monika and James took up a place in the line. Monika was nervous. James appeared calm.

The line moved quickly. Soon Monika and

James were inside the building and waiting to be called:

"Next."

It was their turn.

They both walked up to the wicket. Monika spoke,

"Hi. I've misplaced my key. Could I get my mail from box 1021." Monika flirted with the clerk.

The clerk who had been writing and not paying much attention looked up and was unusually attentive. He seemed a little surprised.

"Box 1 0 2 1?"

"Yeah. I can't find my key. It's not lost. I just misplaced it. I'm sure I'll find it in the next few days." she played the absent minded female role well.

The clerk tried to conceal his sudden nervous look and after some consideration responded,

"Yes Ma'am. I can do that for you. Please wait."

The clerk turned and went out of sight behind the counter to the boxes. Once out of sight of James and Monika he pulled out a small two way radio.

"They're here standby." He put the radio away, went to the box and took something out of it.

After several moments the clerk returned to the

counter. Monika was getting fidgety.

"Here you are. One letter."

He handed the letter to Monika, and gave her a knowing smile, though she did not realize what he had done. Written upon it, in familiar blue ink was: *To Box 1021*. Monika became excited.

"Thank you." she took the envelop and then proceeded with James away from the wicket and to the outside. They were carefully watched by the clerk as they went.

"Next." was called out as they left the Post Office.

They walked closely together and headed between the Post Office and the Bookstore to a bench by a raised garden. They did not notice the reappearance of the two men in the dark suits behind them. Monika was opening the envelope as they walked, ripping it with her index finger along its sealed edge. She opened it and looked in.

"It's empty. There's nothing here."

"What?" James seemed disappointed.

"It's empty. There's nothing in the envelop."

"Here let me look."

Monika passed the envelop over.

Just as James grabbed hold of the envelop, the two men came upon them and pressed concealed guns into their backs,

"I'll take that." the larger of the two said.

"Hey! What's going on." Monika became verbose.

There was a scuffle as the two men pressed Monika and James towards the back of the buildings, where a large dark car was waiting with its engine running in the delivery bay of the Bookstore.

"Get in. Both of you."

James and Monika were quickly forced to the car. The rear passenger door was opened. The thinner man got in first, followed by James and Monika who were being pushed by the larger man to get inside. James tried to fight back, but was quickly restrained.

"Ow. Hey. Watch out!" Monika struggled as she was shoved inside. She grabbed at the large man, caught and ripped his jacket pocket before being pushed inside the car. A small package fell unnoticed from the torn pocket to the roadside.

"Bitch." the man swore and hit her as he got in behind her.

The door closed. Monika and James were both sandwiched tightly inside the car between the two suited men. A third man (the driver) was sitting in front waiting for orders. Two guns were waved at the captives. There was nothing Monika or James could do. They were overpowered and trapped. Monika looked to James as the large man rustled through the envelop.

"Where is it?" was directed at Monika.

"Where's what?" Monika was cocky.

The large man pistol whipped her face.

"Don't even think of it." warned the slighter man who was restraining James in place as he tried to come to Monika's aid.

Blood began to appear on her left cheek.

"You'd better watch your manners, Missy. I'll ask you once more. What was inside here?" the large man displayed the empty envelop as he spoke.

Monika was comforting her wound as she angrily, but cautiously responded,

"In the envelop?"

The man made a hitting motion. Monika cowered.

"Don't play stupid with me. This ain't no game." he waved the weapon menacingly in front of her face. "How would you like a more permanent lesson? Or maybe I should give your *boyfriend* the lesson?"

Monika was quick and compliant in her reply. She did not want James to be hurt,

"There was nothing. It was like that when I

opened it."

"Yeah. Sure." he slapped her with his other hand.

"It was. I swear. Please stop!" Monika went limp as the man grabbed on to her shoulders and shook her,

"Where is it!" he was more threatening.

Just at that instant the rear passenger door opened abruptly. A big burley man in blue jeans was pointing a large gun, which was cocked and aimed at the larger man,

"Freeze!"

Everyone in the car froze.

"Drop them."

The two men in the rear seat dropped their weapons and raised their hands.

"You....Get out." he was indicating Monika and James.

"I hope you know…" the larger man was calm.

"Shut up." he cut off the larger man.

Monika was slow to react at first, not being sure which of these men was safer to be with.

"Come on! Move." he was gruff.

Reacting, Monika climbed over the larger man to get out. As she climbed out the door she stumbled to the ground. The burly man bent to stop her fall in a reflex action, lowering his gun away from the two men inside the car in the process.

"Get out of here. Step on it." was shouted from the back seat.

The car wheels squealed as the driver threw the car into drive. As the car pulled forward the rear passenger door was slammed shut by the sudden forward momentum. The big burley man tried to get Monika out of his way. He stood up and aimed his weapon. The car sped off. He fired two shots at them, but they missed their mark. Monika was on the ground cowering and in distress she cried,

"James! They've got James."

The burley man turned back to Monika and started to help her from the pavement.

As he helped Monika up, he saw a package of matches. He picked it up and read the name. He recognized the name of the bar. It was in North Beach. He smiled,

"Don't worry Miss. Queller. He'll be okay. We'll get him."

"Who are you? How do you know my name?"

The man put his hand into his chest shirt pocket, and removed a small black wallet.

"Bill Meyers, Agent Bill Meyers, FBI."

Monika was stunned.

"Are you alright?" Meyers asked.

"Yes. Yes. I don't understand."

"Will you come with me? I know someone who wants to meet you."

"Where?"

"Will you come?" he repeated.

"Okay." Monika had no other choice if she wanted to save James.

A small crowd had formed nearby and Agent Meyers wanted to get away before the Campus Police became involved. Unbeknownst to him, amongst the crowd was the man who had followed James and Monika from the Aloha Motel. This man was being careful, not wanting to be recognized. He kept out of their sight. He watched as Meyers helped Monika up, and the two of them walked away to the Main Quad.

Chapter 5

"Ah!" James moaned as his body went limp and he slumped down, but only his head rolled forward. His arms and legs were tightly fastened to a wood chair with old thick hemp rope. He felt the tightness of the restriction against him. His chest had two strips of the rope wrapped around him binding him tightly to the chair back. His feet were bound to the chair legs and his hands were secured behind his back. There was much discomfort. He was unable to move freely. He was sweating and worn. The ordeal had been going on for quite some time, though he was not certain how long he had been there. He remembered being blindfolded and having his hands tied soon after his kidnappers had driven away from the university. There had been some rapid conversation between the large and thin man about what they should do. They had decided to blindfold James and continue with their plan.

The trip had taken about forty minutes. James had been able to tell he was in the city by the noises that he had heard as they travelled. Soon the car pulled in somewhere and stopped. He was pulled out. He recalled walking through a doorway into a building and then going up stairs. He was brought into a room and roughly seated and bound to it. After he was secured, his blindfold had been removed. It was a smoke filled room.

The torture had then begun. It had continued for a long time. Now he was exhausted and could not take much more of this abuse.

He lifted his head and looked around. The room was dark and his vision, as a result, tunnel like. One light bulb with an old metallic dark shade was suspended above and spot lit him in the center of an otherwise vacant room. He was not able to see any more of his captors, but he could sense them. James knew someone was there, he could smell the stale odor of their cigarette smoke.

"No more." he mumbled to the emptiness ahead of him.

He was being beaten. There was no rest. Two of his captors were taking turns at him. A slap across the face; a punch to the stomach; a whacking of his head with a belt of some kind. He was sore and bruised. No questions had been asked of him up to this point. He was being prepared.

"What do you want?" there was a tone of beligerence in James' voice as he spoke out into the darkened room.

After several more hits, a voice shot out of the darkness,

"Enough."

The two men who were taking turns beating James backed away from him and into the concealment of the dark room. James now felt very isolated and vulnerable. Blood was dripping from the corner of his mouth, and his left eye was badly bruised and swollen. The light above him was blinding, causing him to squint. Still, he tried to see where the men had gone to and where the voice had come from, but he was not able to break through the intense spotlight and the darkness beyond.

"Who are you?" the voice shot out of the dark.

In pain and disoriented, James directed his reply to where he thought the voice had come,

"James Anstey."

"What are you to the girl?" the voice now came from behind James and startled him. He tried to turn towards it but was prevented from doing so by his restraints.

"Girl?"

The two men walked out of the darkness and grabbed James by his shirt. They prepared to strike him. James cowered, and blurted out,

"You mean Monika?"

"Yes. Ms. Queller." the voice now came from another direction, "Mr. Anstey this will be a lot more efficient if you answer my questions immediately. Please don't make me repeat them or I will have to hurt you again."

James was let go. He slumped back into the chair. The two men once more walked into the darkness of the room. The severity of the beating was more than James had expected.

"Now let's try this again. Why were you with Monika Queller?"

"Ah...I...work with her. We were coming to Palo Alto ...fo...for a trip."

A new man came in from out of the dark room, and struck James hard into his belly and then disappeared back into dark concealment.

"Ugh." James let out in pain.

"I thought we agreed you were not going to make me repeat my questions. I hope another lesson isn't required. Now once again. Why were you with Ms. Queller?" the voice was slow and enunciated each word distinctly.

James understood that there was no point in concealing whatever he knew. They would eventually beat it out of him. His only chance of surviving this was to cooperate to a point. If he was of value to these men, then he might be able to use it to his advantage. He started to speak,

"We…found a note. Monika found it. It was from her father. It said to come to Palo Alto. To go to the university Post Office. To collect something…but it wasn't there." he added quickly

"Collect what?" again the voice came from a new direction.

"I don't know." James was pleading. "She didn't say. I didn't read it. I was driving. It just said… Go to…to the Post Office and get the stuff from box 1021. That was it."

There was a long pause. James was nervous and kept moving his head around staring into the darkness, anticipating a resumption of the beatings.

After several moments, a different voice broke from the dark. It was not aimed at James,

"There wasn't nothin' on him, Boss. There wasn't nothin' on him."

There was a long pause. James waited to hear the response. When none immediately followed, he interrupted.

"What are you going to do with me?"

There was another pause and then from the darkness in front of him came:

"Just keep answering my questions, and you'll be taken care of."

●

A couple of hours later high up in the TransAmerica building, the door to an office opened. An official looking man was holding the handle of the now wide open door and extending a friendly but formal greeting,

"Ms. Queller. Monika. Can I call you Monika? Please. Please come on in. Bill. Please join us. Sorry to keep you waiting so long, but I had to go out of the office." Letting go of the handle, he used hand and arm motions as he spoke. His voice was slow and he enunciated each word distinctly. It was the same voice that had been interrogating James only a short time ago, but neither Meyers nor Monika knew this fact.

Monika entered first and was followed by Agent Meyers. Once they were in, Agent Meyers closed the door after him. They had just come from the lunch room. After Meyers had rescued Monika from the car at the university, he had brought her here to meet his superior. Upon arriving, they were told that they would have to wait. While they waited, Meyers decided to get Monika's cuts and scrapes attended to and something to eat. It had been an unusually long time to wait for his superior, but there had been no other choice. Meyers was displeased, but did not show it. He did not like his superior and this was just another irritant added to the already long list of animosities between the two men.

"Have a seat." The well dressed man in his forties beckoned them towards two chairs that were in front of a large rosewood desk. Through the large office window behind the desk was a magnificent view of the Bay area. It was a clear and sunny day.

As they both sat down, the well dressed man sat down into a chair facing them from the other side of the desk. He had his back to the view. He sat into his chair and entwined the fingers of his hands together, and held them in front of his lowered face as he observed Monika. This gave him a more pensive appearance. For Monika's benefit he then introduced himself,

"I'm Mical Grai. I'm in charge of the San Francisco," he stumbled for the right choice of word, "office."

"Office? What office? I don't understand."

"FBI." Grai looked at Agent Meyers in surprise and then went back to Monika.

"Well Monika," Grai became puzzled in his tone. "I thought you knew about the FBI involvement in your father's case. At least, I thought you understood what was going on. This changes things a bit."

"What do you mean? What's going on here? First I'm followed. Then I'm chased, and James... What are you going to do about James?" Monika was angry, confused and afraid, all at the same time. "Where is he? Who were those men?"

The long wait for Grai had also irritated Monika. She did not like the idea that so much time had been wasted. He seemed so cavalier about the whole situation. She didn't like it.

"Don't worry." Agent Meyers put a comforting hand on her shoulder. "He'll be safe."

"It's not him that they want." Grai was staring right at her. It was uncomfortable for Monika. His words were icy.

"Who's *they*, and what do *they* want? What's going on here?" She was uncomfortable.

Grai changed his demeanor, and rocked forward on his chair unclasping his hands.

"Do you have any idea what your father was working on at the university?"

"Not entirely, but it had something to do with some sort of acceleration experiments. A new form of…ah…something or other."

"Not quite." Grai grinned. "It's classified. Even I don't know all the details. All I can tell you is that he was working for the military. On an advanced technology. A break through. I don't know much more. Only that he *is* the only scientist knowledgeable in this field."

Monika noticed Grai's mistake in referring to her father in the present tense, but let it pass.

"An area that will revolutionize the world. Take us through the next quantum leap, miles ahead of any one else. In the last few days when he was getting close to finishing, that's when he …ah…"

"Died." she finally corrected.

"No Ms. Queller. I don't believe he is dead. I think your parents might be alive."

"What?! Alive? What do you mean? Where are they?"

"They weren't killed. They weren't in an accident. At least as far as I can tell"

"What do you mean?" she repeated. The meaning of these words from Grai hadn't completely sunk into her now pounding head.

"Where are they!?"

"That's the problem." Grai outstretched his arms and included Meyers in his glance. "We don't know. We had hoped that you did." Grai stopped speaking and stared at Monika as if she had some information that he wanted to hear from her. Information that he believed she was keeping secret.

Meyers interrupted the stare,

"We're not entirely sure who is involved. It could be a number of people, but there haven't been any ransom demands or any trace of your parents since the 'accident'. That makes us think they are alive." Meyers interjected in a more sympathetic tone, and then let Grai continue.

"Yes. There had been a security concern from the beginning of the project, but we thought that was all under control. Your father was at the final stage of the project. Just at that last critical stage he disappeared, and all his notes were gone as well."

"What about the accident?"

"I don't know. It is all very unusual." Grai was

being truthful.

"I thought that they'd been lost in the accident. I thought that they'd been swept out, out into the ocean. I believed that they were lost in the surf after their car went over the cliff; that their bodies were pulled out by the current to deeper water. But you're saying that maybe they're okay? That none of that happened?" Monika brightened.

"We never recovered bodies from the car, and we never found any other trace of them. That's what makes us believe that they are alive." Grai was somber.

"You knew this all along?"

"Yes. I'm sorry. We thought it would be wiser not to mention this fact. We didn't know what had happened to them. We've been trying to find them ever since."

Monika sat speechless.

Grai continued,

"We've been keeping track of you. We know about your recent 'problems'. When they started happening, we figured that this was really our first break in the case. We didn't want to take any chances with anything that might lead us to new information. What led you back to Palo Alto?"

"Somebody has been stalking me. You're men?" she asked Grai.

"No. It isn't any of my men. That's why we are interested." Grai answered.

Monika continued,

"I found a note in my father's briefcase..."

"NOTE?"

"Yeah. Here I'll show it to you."

Monika began to go through her briefcase. Grai and Agent Meyers looked on. She pulled out a crumpled envelop with the note half exposed. She handed it to Grai. Grai was intrigued. He took hold of the envelop being offered to him and immediately pulled the rest of the note from inside the envelop. He read it quickly.

"Hum... I see."

"You...you guys didn't know about this?"

"No. No. We had no idea." Grai looked up from reading the note and passed it to Meyers as he asked the next obvious question,

"What was in Box 1021?"

"Nothing. Just an empty envelop, and that's when those guys came up to us and...then Agent Meyers showed up."

"Hum ah." Grai was in thought. He recognized the phone number in the note, but didn't let on that it was familiar to him.

Agent Meyers, now remembering the episode at the university Post Office, put his hand into his pocket and removed the match box that he had found on the ground.

"They dropped this." He handed the match box to Grai.

"The 'Yard'." Grai spoke out loud as he took the match box and read the name that was written upon the flap. "North Beach." He gave Agent Meyers a questioning stare, "We'd better check this out."

"What about my parents? Where are they?"

"I'm sorry Ms. Queller, but I don't know. We haven't got any leads. They've just totally disappeared, along with their research data. It's vital that we get this information back. We had hoped you could help us."

Monika did not respond. She was dazed. It was clear that she would not be able to help. Grai realizing this, abruptly changed his tact,

"Look. Why don't you wait here a moment? Give yourself a chance to take all of this in. Would you like a coffee?"

"Yes. Thank you." Monika was tired and bewildered by all that was happening.

"Cream? Sugar?"

"Yes. Yes please."

Grai moved from behind the desk, and as he passed Monika he gestured for Meyers to follow him. Agent Meyers understood and silently rose to follow after him. After they had both left the room Grai asked,

"Is she straight? Does she know more?"

"Yes. I think that's everything she knows." Meyers was not so certain but he did not let his doubt show in his answer.

"What about this James?"

"Just a boyfriend, sir. Nothing more."

"Okay." Grai being satisfied, quickly changed his mood, "You get her the coffee. I'm going to make a couple of quick calls. I want to check something out. Just to be on the safe side."

Meyers remained for a moment as Grai went on down the hall. Meyers watched as Grai walked away, then he himself turned and went the opposite direction down the hall to get the coffee.

Grai walked further along before turning into a small alcove in the hallway. He checked behind him and seeing no one, pulled a cellular phone out from his jacket pocket. He pressed a key on the phone pad and the phone fast dialed the preset number. Grai put the phone to his ear and nervously waited for an answer. The number rang three times, then was picked up,

"Yeah."

"Everything is fine. He's just the boyfriend.

She's here. How is he?"

There was a confident answer given by the other party. Grai was pleased. Keeping his voice down in the alcove, he ordered,

"Keep him out of sight."

"That should be easy." The man laughed at the other end.

"Don't make any stupid moves." Grai's tone sobered the other man.

"No one can find him here. Boss. Not *even* the FBI." was sarcastically replied.

"Really. They found some matches. One of you idiots must have dropped them. So now they are onto you."

There was a silence on the other end as the other man comprehended the mistake. He then became nervous and asked,

"So, what do you want us to do? Move him?"

"No. Keep him there. I'll keep them away. I'll think of something. Just follow the plan."

"What about her old man?"

"She doesn't know much. At least that's what she's saying. I don't know. It's hard to believe. Set it up. This afternoon." Grai disconnected the call without waiting for a response. He put the phone back into his pocket and took a deep breath.

Everything was proceeding better than he had

planned. In a very short time it would all be over. His associate, though not as trained as his FBI agents, would be able to handle the situation. He had spent a long time in recruiting him and two others to assist in his plan of obtaining and selling Monika's father's work. They were petty criminals and could not be linked to him. In his position as FBI Bureau Chief he felt protected. No-one would be able to uncover this subterfuge, and when or if they did, he would be far away and wealthy. No-one would find him. He composed himself and then turned from his alcove position and headed back up the hallway to his office to rejoin Monika and Meyers.

●

Far below, from outside the TransAmerica building on the street, a man in a dark car was looking up through his windshield as he spoke on a cell phone.

"Yeah. She's in the building. In Grai's office."

On the seat next to the man, there was a two way radio device. It was listening into the conversation in Grai's office. The conversation was taking his attention from his phone call.

"I'll call you back. They're back in the office now."

●

High above and back in the TransAmerica building Grai was now coming into his office. Meyers had not yet returned.

"What about James?" Monika was asking of Grai as he re-entered the office.

Their conversation continued,

"Don't worry Monika, he'll be okay. We'll get him. I've already put some of our agents on to it." Grai crossed the room and sat down in the seat behind his desk.

"Is there any possibility that…this note;" he picked up the note and showed it to her, "that there was anything else in your father's briefcase? Did you check it?"

"Yes I did."

"Where is the briefcase now?"

"It's in James' car. At the university."

"The university?"

"It's still parked there. I didn't go back there. I was brought right here."

"I see."

At that moment the door to the office opened. Agent Meyers had returned with the coffee. He entered the room and distributed the cups to each of them, and then sat down in his original seat.

"Thank you." Monika took the warm drink.

"You're welcome." Meyers smiled.

Grai picked up his cup and nodded his thanks to Meyers. As he sipped, he began to rise up from his chair,

"Excuse me a moment."

This startled both Meyers and Monika.

Grai noticed and tried to jokingly excuse himself to the men's room,

"I'll be right back."

Meyers and Monika were stone faced as Grai crossed the room and went out of the office, closing the door after him. He again walked a little way down the hall and after several steps he pulled out his cellular phone. There was no one else in the hall. He speed dialed a number. Grai did not wait, but quickly spoke into the phone upon its being answered,

"Okay. It's in the briefcase. I'm going to get it now. Say you'll trade the guy for the briefcase. At Ghirardelli. Tonight. At seven. Do it now."

Grai hung up. He was pleased. Things were falling into place. He walked back to his office, opened the door, but before he entered composed himself. He then re-entered, crossed the room, and sat down behind his desk. His plan was about to unfold.

"Sorry about that." Grai was about to continue when his office phone rang.

"Excuse me." He answered his phone. It was his secretary. She sounded alarmed. Grai understood.

"Yeah." Grai listened. "Put it through. And try and get a trace. I'm putting it on the speaker."

Grai pushed the button on his speaker phone and put the receiver back into its cradle. A man's voice emanated from the speaker.

"I understand you're looking for someone. A Mr. Anstey?"

"Who is this?" Grai demanded. Monika rose from her seat upon the mentioning of James' name.

"It doesn't matter. Don't bother trying to trace this. Just listen. We want the briefcase."

"What briefcase?" Grai was being coy, and privately with hand motions, directed both Meyers and Monika to remain silent.

"You know. Seven PM sharp. Fisherman's Wharf. Ghirardelli building."

Monika could not hold her silence any longer and called out loud,

"James?"

"Be there." A click then sounded over the speaker phone that was followed by the dial tone.

There was a silent pause and a look of apprehension on Monika's face. Grai asked,

"What do you make of that Meyers?"

"I don't know. That's pretty sudden."

"They'd know we'd be involved. Especially after the university."

"Yeah. You're right. Still…" Meyers was perplexed. He hadn't expected to receive a call so soon with regard to James' abduction.

Grai picked up the phone and rang through to his secretary,

"Did you get anything?"

The secretary's answer was obvious from the feigned look of disappointment on Grai's face.

"Thanks." Grai hung up and then directed his words to Meyers. "We weren't on long enough. Let's take Miss. Queller and go to the car at the university. We'll get the briefcase and see if there is anything else in it. There's not much else we can do until seven. Maybe this will all be over quickly and safely after the exchange. Miss. Queller you must be hungry. We'll get something to eat."

"We had something earlier, while we were waiting." Meyers informed Grai.

"Good." Grai acknowledged.

"What if they know about the car and…" Meyers was worried.

"If they already had the case they wouldn't have exposed themselves to us now. It must still be in the car. We'd better get going." Grai moved from behind the desk and ushered both Monika and Meyers out of the office.

●

Down below in the car on the street, the man who had been listening to the office conversation was now speaking on his cellular phone,

"Yeah. It's set up. Ghirardelli. Seven. I have the briefcase."

"..
.............................."

"Okay. Be ready. I think this is it."

He hung up the phone and smiled. He would wait till Monika exited the building and then continue to tail her as per his orders.

●

James was still bound to the chair in the interrogation room. The blinding beam of light was still coming from high above him. He was still not able to make out anything beyond its glare. He was tired and afraid. His body hurt from his abductors abuse. He was bruised. His cheeks were swollen from the hard fists that had hit him. He didn't understand what this was all about. It seemed far more brutal and intense than it should have been, or at least as he thought it should have been. It was far more horrifying.

He was now alone in the room. His abductors had all left a short while ago. He wasn't certain as to how long it had been, as his sense of time was disoriented. Before they had left, someone had again blindfolded him. James thought that this meant that he was about to meet his death. He had remained silent during the blindfolding and did not give any fight. It would have been pointless. His hands and legs were still securely tied to the chair. If he struggled he would merely topple to the floor still attached to the chair. As a result, he would become greatly immobilized and even more vulnerable to the whim of his captors. He was perspiring with fear as he awaited what was about to happen to him. His senses were heightened. He could smell, sense and hear much better. He wondered why he was in this situation. It was not as it should have been.

There were several moments of apprehension upon being tied and blindfolded. He waited. James heard the door open. To his surprise he heard the shuffling of footsteps going away, not towards him. It was followed by the sound of the door closing. The room was now quiet and still. He strained his hearing, searching for any sound that might be a confirmation of what he believed had just happened, but there was not a sound. No one was in the room with him. He now realized that the purpose of his being blindfolded again was to prevent him from identifying any of his abductors as they had opened the door to the room and left. Once that door was opened, James correctly surmised, there would have been a burst of light that would have illuminated the room and then revealed the identity of the man who had been interrogating him.

After several more minutes of anticipation, James was satisfied that he had been left alone; that for the moment he was in no danger. His body was tense, but he felt the elation of this reprieve. It did not last long. He became acutely aware of his aches and pains from the beatings. He let out a sigh, sensing that he was securely alone. He could not go on much longer. He hoped someone, anyone, would come and rescue him— but how? When? He felt the dry caked blood on the skin of his face. He slumped his head forward. He was emotionally worn and physically exhausted. He wondered what was to become of him.

●

Grai, Meyers and Monika all left through the large main entrance of the TransAmerica building together. They did not suspect that they were being watched. They appeared to be in no hurry.

They crossed over the sidewalk to where Meyers had parked his car on the street. Monika had not noticed before that Meyers had parked in a reserved zone. There was a small sign that indicated this spot was reserved for official vehicles. Meyers opened the rear door of the car for Monika. She thanked him and got into the car. He closed the door after her and then crossed around to the driver's side, opened that door and got in behind the steering wheel. Grai opened and got into the front passenger seat. When the lane was clear, Meyers pulled the car out into the road and drove on.

All of this was being observed from a distance by a man in a car a hundred feet or so up the street. After Meyers had pulled out, the man watching also started his car and pulled out to follow after them. He was not noticed amongst all the other traffic.

Inside their car, nothing was being said between Meyers, Grai or Monika. They rode on in silence as the street sights and sounds of the big city passed by them. The streets were not very busy. Up and down the picturesque streets of San Francisco they went, soon making their way from downtown onto the freeway heading south for Stanford University. As they progressed they were still unaware of their being followed. Behind them several hundred feet, a dark sedan had copied their every move.

It was a scenic drive on the 280 freeway through the foothills south from San Francisco to Palo Alto. Monika loved this area. It was heaven on earth to her. She had spent some of the most memorable moments of her life in the Bay area. It was the only place in all of her travels that reminded her of being at home. The sky was the most clear blue and the sun was warm upon her. The sweet smell of eucalyptus was everywhere. It was a typical California day.

As they continued to drive, Monika reminisced about her parents and family life before all of the recent strangeness. She missed those days and desperately wanted to return to them. With Grai's belief that her parents were not dead, Monika had found a glimmer of a new joy within her. Being back in San Francisco was not the horrific experience she had anticipated. There was now a sense of hope and possibility. Somewhere her parents were alive. Somewhere in this area they were waiting to be found and rescued. She hoped they were safe. She looked forward to seeing them and being reunited with a life that she had believed was forever lost. It had been so lonely without her family. She wanted to believe that they were alive. Were they *really* safe? Was this all just a dream? She was confused. No, it couldn't be. Here she was in a car, with these men. They were alive. They must be. She was elated and then angered. Why had she been put through all of this agony? Why? Monika silently shook her head as the car drove on. She had so many questions.

They had continued on in silence till about twenty minutes later. Meyers had come to the turn off for the university. He announced:

"It won't be long now."

They exited the freeway and got onto Sand Hill Road. Monika knew this area like the back of her hand. They were almost at their destination. They would be at the northern entrance to the university in ten minutes. Being in the university area again, Monika's thoughts turned to James and the events at the Post Office. She prayed James would be alright. She didn't want to go through the same pain as when she had lost her parents.

Gradually they made their way on down the winding roadway and to the outskirts of the campus. Once at the outskirts just before the Stanford Shopping Mall, Meyers turned onto Junipero Serra Boulevard and took the back way leading via Los Arboles Avenue, to Santa Teresa Street, to

Panama Street, to Campus Drive, to Palm Drive. Enroute they passed Lake Lagunita and in minutes the Hoover Tower and the university came into view, with its sturdy sandstone buildings and terra cotta roofs. They were there.

It was now the early afternoon, there were many more people coming and going on foot and riding their bikes about the paths and roads of the campus. Meyers slowed down as he turned and approached the Main Quadrangle and the place where James and Monika had parked the car. Monika had moved forward to the edge of the rear seat and was now sitting upright looking through the front windshield between Meyers and Grai. She watched as they neared the place where James' car was parked.

"There." she pointed. "There." she focused Meyers and Grai towards James' car. "There it is there. The red one."

"Oh yeah. I see it." Meyers acknowledged.

"Pull up there." Grai indicated, "Next to it. That empty space." Grai indicated the space adjacent to the car.

Meyers made his way over to the space. He pulled in and parked next to the Corvette. He turned the car's engine off.

"Well. Let's see what we can find." Meyers

announced indicating that it was time to investigate.

Monika was first to get out. Followed quickly by Grai and then Meyers. Monika stood for a moment and looked James' car over. It appeared to be untouched from when it had been left there earlier that morning.

"Where did you put it?" Grai asked.

"Right over here." Monika spoke as she moved to the passenger side of the red convertible and leaned over to search behind the passenger seat. "It is right here. I put it right…"

Monika was now looking for the briefcase, but was not able to find it. She leaned over to search behind the driver's seat, but still did not find it.

"I put it right here. I'm sure." Monika was perplexed. "It's gone."

"Gone?" Grai spoke as he regarded Meyers with astonishment.

Grai moved closer to her and waited as Monika searched behind the passenger seat of the car. Finding nothing, she expanded her search to the rear compartment of the car on both sides. The briefcase was not to be found. She stood back up and faced Grai and Meyers.

"It's not here? Someone's taken it. Someone has taken my father's briefcase."

Grai frowned a look of disbelief,

"That's going to complicate things."

"Complicate?" Monika didn't like the sound of Grai's comment. "What's going to happen?"

"Don't be worried Ms. Queller. We'll work something out for tonight. We'll still do the exchange. We'll just have to get a dummy brief-case that matches your father's." Meyers reassured.

"Yes." Grai joined in. "Don't worry. It'll be fine. We'll get another case. No one will know the difference, and once the exchange is done...It won't matter. Your friend will be okay. Let's go back to the office and get things organized for tonight's meeting. We can make all the necessary arrangements."

Monika nodded her agreement. She was disappointed that the briefcase had been taken. She felt a great sentimental loss.

"Get someone over here to look after this." Grai spoke to Meyers indicating James' car.

"Right." Meyers acknowledged.

They all walked back and got into the car. They would leave James' car where it was. There was no need to move it. It would be safe.

Meyers started their car, pulled out of the parking space, and drove off. A hundred feet away another car started up and followed after them.

Chapter 6

At the same time that Monika, Meyers and Grai were examining James' parked car at the university, on the far side of San Francisco, a dark late model four door sedan was pulling up in front of a North Beach bar. The sedan pulled up to the curb on the opposite side of the street in a no parking zone. It was a fairly busy day. There were many shoppers and tourists walking along the sidewalks.

The car stopped. Four men in dark suits got out and quickly huddled together on the sidewalk facing the bar. Once a few words had been spoken,

one of the men, who was tall and blond, turned
back to the car, leaned over and briefly spoke to
the driver. When he had finished, he stood
upright, turned and gave his attention to his associates on the sidewalk. As the men resumed conversation, the car pulled away and almost immediately made a 'U' turn back towards the bar,
heading for its parking lot.

The 'Yard' was on a corner. It was a dilapidated
two story building. An old neon sign, half illuminated, was precariously hanging over its front
entrance atop two dirty stainless steel doors. It
was a trendy part of town, but this particular street
was still unchanged from its earliest days. The
'Yard' was a local bar not intended for the tourist
trade. In its day it had been a popular place, but
now it was rough and uninviting.

The blond man continued to speak to his associates. They were discussing final arrangements
and making sure that the 'Yard' was quiet. After a
few moments they all broke from their union.
Two of the men walked away from the others and
crossed over to the right side of the bar heading
for the back exit. The blond and his other remaining associate carefully dodged the cars and
crossed the street directly in front of the bar. Once
across, they waited on the sidewalk in front of the

bar trying not to look suspicious. This would give the others time to get into their positions. No customers were going in or out of the bar.

The blond man checked his wristwatch. It was time to make their move. The two men made their way directly into the bar and entered from the bright daylight into its darkness. The sudden darkness heightened their senses. They paused for a moment in the entrance. They heard the noise of music and smelt the smoky, boozy, bawdy aroma of the place. They stood inside at the entrance for a few moments, and soon began to make out the interior of the bar. It did not take them long to adjust to the change of light.

Being mid afternoon the 'Yard' was pretty dead. On their left side was the bar running the length of the place. To their right was a small dance floor with an old disco ball suspended over a ten by ten raised hardwood dance floor. There was a low brass railing around the dance floor and a brass pole going from ceiling to floor in the farthest corner. It was obviously used during the strip tease that was a regular feature here in the bar, but was now vacant.

The name: 'Yard', referred to this brass railed in dance floor. Many little upright pieces of brass were fixed in place, giving the railing a resemblance of a picket fence without the points. A jukebox stood at the far wall loudly playing a country western song. Many circular tables and chairs were scattered throughout the remaining space of the room. One sole male patron, seated at one of the tables near the 'Yard', was nursing a beer and paid absolutely no attention to their entry.

Behind the bar was the bartender, who had looked up to see who had entered, and had begun to approach the new patrons from behind his bar. The bartender was in shirt sleeves rolled up to his mid arm. He was an insipid long haired man in his thirties. He was drying a glass with a soiled cloth. The two men went to the bar and sat upon stools. The blond sat facing the bar, and his associate was turned facing the room.

"What can I get you?" the bartender asked without moving closer.

"Two beers." the blond was gruff.

The bartender didn't ask what type. He just repeated the order,

"Two beers." and then stopped his drying and turned down to the beer refrigerator to get two beers.

As the two men sat at the bar waiting for their drinks, the blond kept his eyes on the bartender, while the other reconnoitered the room. At the far end of the bar next to the jukebox, there was a corridor. There was a sign indicating the washrooms attached to one of its walls and above the corridor a red neon EXIT sign. There were no other hallways nor exits other than the one through the front metal doors.

The bartender had now returned and put two beers with two glasses on coasters in front of the men.

"That's $5.50."

The blond put his left hand into his pants pocket, pulled out some money, examined it quickly and threw a ten dollar bill onto the bar,

"Keep it."

"Thank you." The bartender was pleased with the tip. He picked up the money and retreated to the far end of the bar where he raised up a section of the counter top and crossed over to the jukebox and interrupted the music by pulling out the plug. The song groaned to a halt. The bartender then crossed back to behind the bar lowering the counter top back into place. He leaned under the counter and fiddled with something. Immediately the Disco Ball was spotlighted above the dance floor, and began turning. As it turned, light cascaded throughout the bar. The show was about to begin.

From the corridor at the back of the bar a young woman came into view. She was very pretty and scantily dressed. Much of her was revealed through her tight clothing. She placed a Boom Box on top of the jukebox and pushed a couple of its buttons. From the Boom Box came the music to which she danced. It was loud and suggestive. The woman walked matter-of-factly over to the dance floor paying little attention to the bar patrons, stepped over the railing and began her routine. The drunk patron at the table near the dance floor paid no attention to the woman or her act, but just sat there and drank. This didn't bother the woman who was in a world of her own as she danced and began to strip using the brass pole as her companion.

The two men took a couple of sips from their drinks as they watched the girl dance, then got up from their stools. They walked to the end of the bar towards the corridor that led to the washrooms and the back exit. The blond called out above the music to the bartender as they approached,

"The can's back there?"

"Yeah. Just around the corner." the bartender was smiling and his eyes were fixed upon the dancer as he answered.

The two men continued walking down the length of the bar and into the corridor that the bartender had indicated led to the washrooms. As they walked into the corridor, the music from the dancer became more distant. Abruptly there was a left turn, and then a shorter hallway and a right turn. At the end of the hall was a locked shut steel door with an illuminated neon EXIT sign above it. The hallway was dimly lit and smelt of smoke and fetid washrooms. On their left side close together, there were two doors each with signs upon them that indicated the male and female washrooms. The doors were dirty with grimy hand prints.

On the opposite side there was a staircase that led upward to the second story and any offices that belonged to the bar. The men walked down this short hallway to the steel door. There was pile of boxes in front of the door. The two men moved the boxes out of the way, keeping an eye out for any type of intruder who might enter into the hallway. When the way was clear, the blond without speaking gestured to his associate to open the back steel door. His partner quickly went over to unlock and open the door. There was a squeak as the door opened. They both froze and hesitated before going any further. The blond looked back towards the bar and waited to see if the noise had been heard above the dancer. They were lucky. No one had heard the noise of the back door opening. He motioned his associate to hurry. All of these events happened smoothly and quickly. They had been well rehearsed. As the door was fully opened it revealed the bright light of the outside.

On the other side of the door lay the rear parking lot to the bar. Waiting just outside were the other two men who had walked around the building. They had not been there long. On crossing the street enroute to the rear lot, these men had been looking for telephone wires. Once around the back of the bar and very close to the rear exit, they had found the phone line. One of the men had, as per orders, taken out a pair of wire snips and severed the connection, thereby isolating the bar from outside contact. It would take at least a day before any repair could be made.

Now that the door was opened, the dark four door sedan could be seen in the parking lot. The blond gestured to the driver that all was going according to plan and that he should keep the car running while he waited. The two men standing by the door outside in the rear lot entered quickly through the opened door into the bar hallway.

They closed the door behind them. Not a word was said amongst the four men inside. They communicated sparingly through gestures. This was obviously a subversive mission of some sort, as evidenced by their each pulling out hand guns with silencers. The blond waved his gun to indicate the commencement of the next stage of the plan. They readied themselves for the onslaught. The tension was high.

The blond gave a few more gestured commands. Two of the men would come with him upstairs, while one would remain here below, on guard. They were nervous and wanted to proceed quickly before they were discovered. They hoped that everything would go well and that there would be no interruptions. The element of surprise was the best weapon they had, and they were not willing to lose this advantage.

Once everything was understood, with the blond in the lead, the three men started up the stairs. The stairs were old and creaked as they placed their weight upon them. They tried to minimize the sound by walking to the outside of the stair boards. They hoped that the distraction of the music of the dancer inside the 'Yard' would be enough to conceal them. They continued with guns drawn, upward.

At the top of the stairs was another hallway. It ran the length of the upper level parallel to the street outside and was more like a landing attached to the stairwell rather than an enclosed hallway. Like the downstairs, it was also dimly lit and dirty. There were no windows to the outside, only three doors, which the blond knew led to the three bar offices. The doors were old and by their appearance were made of wood; each door was closed.

The blond motioned his associates to their positions. Each of the three stealthily arranged themselves near the closed doors to each office. They each waited to one side of their respective doorways. They were not certain as to what they might find inside. The blond took a deep breath and blew it out and then signaled. Each on cue instantly burst into the separate offices with their guns raised at the ready.

The blond's door burst open into a poorly lit office. There was a window with its venetian blinds rolled down. The outside view was totally blocked. Three men, casually sitting around, were abruptly interrupted. One was behind a big desk with his feet upon it; the other two were sitting on a sofa facing the desk. They had all been caught off guard. Upon realizing what was happening, the two on the sofa started to rise up. The man behind the desk fell from his chair, landing onto the floor with a loud snap. One of the rising men put his hand into his coat breast pocket.

"Don't try it." the blond gestured menacingly with his gun.

The man pulled his hand back and raised it up in front of him. He sat back down timidly with the other one on the sofa.

"Get over there with them." The blond directed his attention to the man on the floor behind the desk.

Without questioning, the man rose from the floor and moved over to join the other men on the sofa. When he was seated the blond spoke,

"Put your guns on the floor. Slowly. One at a time. We'll start with you." He pointed to the man on the left end of the sofa.

One by one each of the men removed their weapons. When they had each finished, the blond came closer and with his left foot pushed the guns out of reach of the three of them.

"Good. Now…" he waved his gun in front of them, and took a couple of steps back towards the doorway. "Where is he?"

"Where's who?" the man on the left edge of the sofa smartly answered.

"What is this?" the man in the center spoke right after the other. It was an obvious attempt to create some confusion.

"Where is he?" the blond was more firm.

There was still no answer. Without asking a third time the blond aimed his gun and shot once into the arm of the man who had first answered on the left. The quiet muffled sound of the silenced shot did not leave the room. The man moaned in agony while the other two quickly understood that this blond was to be taken seriously.

"In the second room. We don't know nothing else. We were meant to keep him here. That's all." the man in the center offered without further prompting.

"That's better. Here."

The blond pulled out plastic ties from his left pocket with his free hand and threw them onto the man in the center.

"You know what to do with these."

The center man nodded in understanding. He collected the ties, and proceeded to handcuff himself as well as the other two. As they cuffed themselves the blond backed into the doorway, while keeping his gun aimed at the three men. Everything had gone well so far. They were ahead of schedule. He leaned carefully into the hallway to see the progress of his partners. One of them was just exiting the first office. There was no one with him. He looked over to the blond,

Nothing. The man from the first office put his thumb and index finger together and indicated to the blond that there was nothing inside that office.

Understanding the message, the blond beckoned his associate over. He gestured that he should check after the second man in the second office. The associate nodded his understanding of these orders, and moved down the hall towards the next door.

Just as this silent communication was being completed the second man appeared from the second office. He was not alone. He had James with him. He was helping James out of the office. James seemed disoriented, but was cognizant that he was being rescued. He was eager to get away from this place. He was weak and needed assistance to walk. He was bruised and cut. His clothes were dirty. He was being helped into the hallway and towards the stairs...

...*The second office had no window. Upon bursting in, James' rescuer had seen that it had been boarded up which resulted in making the room very dark and musty. The smell of stale smoke lingered there.*

The only light in the room was coming from a single strong lamp hanging directly over and focused on James, who was seated and tied upon a wood chair. There was no furniture other than the chair that James was tied to and one that was about ten steps in front of him against the wall.

James had anticipated the worst at the sound of the door crashing in. He had believed that this was to be his end. He had not cried out. Instead, he tried to see through the light of the open door. What was going to happen to him? He had earlier managed to loosen the blindfold enough with his facial movements that he could see through a section, but he could not make out who had burst in. There was someone. He tried to make out the figure, but he could only see a silhouette. He strained to make out the figure coming through but it wasn't until he had been asked,

"James?" by the intruder, that he realized that this was someone coming to help him. It was in the way his name had been quietly spoken, that had brought him to this conclusion. He had muttered in a similar low voice,

"Yes. Thank God."

And that was that. The rescuer had come over to James. He had quickly removed the blindfold and untied him. James was weak and not very stable on his legs. The man had helped him to his feet.

"We must hurry. Don't speak. Come with me."
had been said as they made their way to the door
of the office. James had obeyed. With each step he
was getting stronger. He had squinted from the
light while being guided by his rescuer...

Now that they were in the hallway and James saw the other men of the rescue team, he knew that he was going to be safe.

The blond acknowledged James and his associates. He indicated to them to go on downstairs. With James supported between them, the two associates made their way to the stairs. James was safe. The blond turned his attention back to his captives in the office on the sofa,

"Okay. Get up." he motioned the three by pointing his gun as he spoke.

The three cuffed men got up from the sofa and under gun point made their way to the door and out of the office. They immediately saw that their captive had been rescued and understood the predicament that they were now in. They were shuffled down the hall to the stairs. The blond was behind them keeping his gun pointed in their direction. They all went down the stairs and were rustled out of the rear exit and into the lot. No one in the bar below had seen or had been aware of what had happened during the last several minutes. The blond and his men were pleased that it had all gone so smoothly. The steel door was securely closed. They had all made it so far without incidence.

Outside in the parking lot, they did not waste any time. They all quickly went over to and got into their dark sedan. James was put in the front, and the three prisoners were put in the back. It was a tight fit for them all to get in. The doors closed, and the car rapidly pulled out of the lot, driving down the side street, and not passing in front of the bar. As they drove away there was soon no trace that they had ever been there.

Inside the bar, the dancer was just finishing her routine. She was completely nude. The bartender, having been visually satisfied, became curious as to what had happened to the two men. He walked to the end of the bar, lifted the section and went into the corridor to see what had happened to them. He carefully walked down to the washrooms. He slowly opened the Men's Room door. He leaned in and had a look. No one was inside. He closed the door and stood for a moment listening. There wasn't a sound. He noticed that the boxes that he had earlier placed at the back door had been moved. He guessed that the two men must have moved them in order to get access to the back door. They must have left. It was strange, but he didn't care. He was just the bartender; a hired employee, and had no knowledge of what was going on upstairs. He shrugged it off, turned and went back down the hallway to the bar. They had paid for their drinks.

●

Meyers, Grai and Monika arrived back at the TransAmerica building. The drive from the university had been in a different type of silence than the trip down. Monika was concerned that by not finding the briefcase, the hope of finding her parents was now greatly diminished. She was full of worry and was not interested in talking with Grai or Meyers.

Meyers understood how Monika felt. He was a veteran of such missions. He was also worried about what this might mean in terms of successfully completing the mission. He drove without saying a word, though he did from time to time check in his rear view mirror to see that Monika was alright.

Grai was full of thoughts about what had happened to the briefcase. He wondered who had taken it. Was it a stranger? Just a thief passing by, or was it something more? Was this all part of something else? Was it a double cross? He wasn't sure, but there was nothing that he could do about it. He remained silent while he tried to work out all the ramifications of these events. He would make a call when he got back to the office. A call to check that everything was still going according to plan.

It was very late in the afternoon. They were all quietly disappointed. The trip back to San Francisco did not seem to take as long as the trip to Palo Alto. Upon their return to the TransAmerica building Meyers pulled the car over to the entrance to the underground parking of the building. He stopped the car beside a terminal and pushed the button to roll down his window. He then took a plastic credit card out from his sun visor and inserted it into the terminal. The terminal flashed a green light and spit out the card. Meyers took the card and placed it back in its place in the visor. As he did this, the garage doors began to slowly open up. Meyers closed his car window, turned on his headlights and when the garage door was opened enough, he drove forward. They drove down two levels in the concrete lot and finally pulled into the section that was reserved parking for their office.

Meyers stopped the engine and they all got out

of the car. Monika followed Meyers and Grai to the elevator. Grai pushed the call button. The door to the elevator opened and they all got in.

●

On the street outside the TransAmerica building a car pulled up and parked in the same spot as it had earlier been, before it had begun its tail of Meyers, Grai and Monika. It had been a long afternoon. The man in the car pulled out a listening devise and waited.

●

Several minutes later, the sound of an elevator arriving at its floor rang out. From the office hallway could be seen the light indicating the arriving elevator. The two outer steel doors opened. Grai was the first to step from the elevator, followed by Monika and then Meyers. They walked down the hallway towards Grai's office.

Opening the office door, Grai ushered Monika and Meyers in. They proceeded to sit in the same places as earlier that afternoon before they had left for the university.

"Coffee?" Grai remained at the door awaiting their answer. These were the first words that had been spoken since their return trip.

"Yes. Thank you." Monika sounded a little distant. She was staring through the office window as she spoke. The mist was beginning to roll in over the Golden Gate. It was a beautiful calming sight. It looked like a huge cotton batten comforter as it blanketed the Bay in preparation for night fall, and bed. Bed. Monika suddenly felt sleepy.

Meyers, assuming he would be the one to go on the errand for the coffee, began to rise from his seat.

Grai raised his left hand to stop him,

"No. No. You stay there. It's my turn."

Meyers sat back down.

"I won't be long."

Grai turned and left the office to go for the coffee, closing the door behind him. Once he was far enough away, he pulled his cellular phone out from his coat pocket. Opening the phone he pushed a button, and brought the phone to his ear. The phone speed dialed. There was no ring nor any other sound coming forth. Then, after several more seconds an announcement reported:

"The number you have called is temporarily out of service. Please try your call later. Thank you for using…"

Grai disconnected and tried again. After several moments of silence the same announcement was repeated:

"The number you have called is temporarily out of service. Please ..."

Again he disconnected but this time placed the phone back into his pocket. Something was wrong or maybe it was nothing. Maybe the problem with the phone was just a coincidence. He wondered if this had anything to do with the stolen briefcase. He was puzzled, but again realized that there was nothing he could do about it. He hoped that everything was fine and that the trouble with the phone was just a coincidence. He did not have the time to worry about it now. There were many things to do before the exchange. He would try again later, if he could get the chance, but now he had to get the coffee. He did not want to raise any suspicions. There were already enough complications. 'Surely,' he thought, 'everything was going according to plan.' He had expected there would be some minor mishaps. All of these events, though inconvenient, were within the range of expectation. There was no need to cancel what was already in progress. It was too late to consider any rearrangements. There had been far too many months of preparation to terminate now due to these minor events. As he turned to go and get the coffee, he hoped everything would be alright.

Chapter 7

Soaring high above San Francisco looking to the north beyond the Bay area was the most magnificent spectacle. The separation between water and the blue heavens was difficult to distinguish. The sun was setting far away into the fine line of horizon between sky and ocean. The water was calm and yet majestic. From this height a few tiny whitecaps speckled throughout the ocean. The water was mirror like and reflected the brilliance of the day's end. The evening sky colors were incredible in their variety of red, yellow, and violet hues. The sight was heavenly. From far out into the ocean, a giant billowing white mass was gently surfing over the water towards the city. The mountainous land funneled the white mist along its coast and on through the Golden Gate Bridge. Gradually the mist flowed over the bridge and on into the inner bay. The city on its high peaks was surrounded by a soft white. The red spires of the Golden Gate pierced through the white, but that was all that could be seen of its structure. The Bay area was now blanketed by the white mist and tucked in for the night. The land and buildings amidst it, seemed to represent a magical kingdom high in the clouds of a make believe world.

In the heart of this realm and below, near Fisherman's Wharf, a car was making its way down the street and into the fishing harbor area. There were many fishing boats docked. Some were unloading their day's catch and others were returning from a day's rental sport fishing expedition. There was alot of activity in the area. Many tourists were milling around admiring the sights and sounds.

Meyers, Grai and Monika had left the TransAmerica building late. There had been difficulty in finding a replica of Monika's briefcase, but finally they had found one. They now drove quickly through the city streets to their destination; worried that they would not get to the exchange on time.

As they arrived at Fisherman's Wharf, Meyers was lucky to find an available parking spot. He drove in, pulled up and parked in the main lot facing the direction of the red brick Ghirardelli building under the large circular Fisherman's Wharf sign. Grai was seated in front with Meyers, and Monika was in the back. She was a little anxious and fidgety. It had been a long day with many surprises in it. She was tired and a little stunned from all of the events. She was bewildered to be here in this situation. It felt unreal to her; like she was watching a movie that was almost finished. She expected that at any moment the house lights would go up and it would all be over. But it was not a movie and the house lights did not go up. It was real.

The replica of her father's briefcase was by her side on the seat. She patted it to confirm its concreteness and the reality that she was actually here in this place under these circumstances.

Meyers turned out the headlights and stopped the car's engine. There was silence. They all remained in their seats in the dusk of the early evening. The time showing on the car radio was

6:45 PM. In another fifteen minutes it would all be over. They all had pre-performance jitters.

After a suitable amount of time, Grai broke the nervous silence,

"Well, are you ready?" he turned and was speaking to Monika in the back seat.

Monika nodded her head in acknowledgment. She did not speak. She was still in thought. She was nervous but ready. She knew that there was no other avenue available. This was the only way to get him back, and it was imperative for her to get James back safely.

Without further prompting, they each opened their doors and got out of the car. Meyers turned and spoke to Grai over the roof of the car as he closed his door behind him,

"Just in case something goes wrong." He jingled the keys at eye level so that Grai could see. "I have an extra set. Okay?" He tossed the keys over to him.

"Thanks." was all that Grai said.

The three of them crossed through the parking lot. They walked together on the sidewalk that would take them towards the Ghirardelli building. Monika was carrying the briefcase. Each of them was scanning the area around and ahead, keeping an eye out for anything suspicious. It was difficult however, to identify anything unusual as the area was crowded and noisy with tourists.

They kept a quick pace, heading for the Ghirardelli building and the exchange. They were not far from their destination. As they approached, Grai was becoming uneasy. He wondered if there was anything wrong; if there was anything he should or could do. He had been unable to go and investigate for himself; not having an opportunity to get away from Meyers and Monika. He hadn't been able to make contact with his associates, eventhough he had attempted through telephoning. Resultantly, there had been no chance to properly re-evaluate. He had an unsettled feeling that he couldn't explain.

Grai wanted the briefcase. He hadn't anticipated its mysterious loss. He had originally expected that the exchange would indirectly deliver it to him via his associates, and it would then all be over, no-one would suspect his involvement, but that plan was no longer of any use. He accepted that there was nothing to do at this point but to go on. Go on and play this hand through. It was only a few more yards. Only a few more minutes. He couldn't allow his uneasiness to affect him. The events were in motion and any change this late in the game would only cause more difficulties;

would only raise suspicions. It was not the time to act irrationally. The best path was to follow the plan already set out. If anything went wrong, he would deal with it at that moment. Once the exchange was completed, he could regroup—then, when he eventually discovered the whereabouts of the real briefcase, he would re-establish his priorities. He could consider other plans and put them into execution. For the time being, he had to follow through on the existing chain of events, or risk revealing himself and losing everything he had strived so hard to achieve. Still, Grai found himself regretting that he had not been able to communicate with his associates. To reassess the situation and make any necessary changes. To cancel the exchange if the situation warranted. 'If only…' he thought, but the moment was upon him. There was no turning back.

They walked on and followed the path. After a couple of minutes, they found themselves in front of the Ghirardelli building, the trendy small tourist Mall. They stopped ten feet in front of the building to examine the area before proceeding. There was nothing of note, just more tourists. Grai motioned Meyers to go ahead. With Monika in front, they crossed over and entered into the Mall through its main glass doors.

The Mall had been created out of the old reconditioned chocolate factory. All of the interior walls had been exposed and were sandblasted back to their original glaze. It had created a very attractive warehouse effect to the Mall. The ceiling was high, giving a feeling of openness and there were many shops created out of the nooks and crannies of the old refurbished factory. There were several plaques upon the walls outlining the historic background of the building. Large blown up black and white enlargements of old yellowed photographs hung upon the walls, creating a pictorial view to the written past referred to upon the plaques.

They walked a few yards further into the Mall and stopped to one side of the entrance out of the immediate traffic of the shoppers to the various boutiques. It was very busy for a Saturday evening, and though they were off to one side, it was difficult to keep out of the way of the stream of passers by. The three were forced farther back to the wall. They were pushed tightly together. Monika was held sandwiched by Grai and Meyers. They all nervously waited.

Meyers checked his watch: 6:59 PM. It would be anytime now. He turned his vision to the Mall and the main thoroughfare that ran directly in front of them and off about fifty feet. There were quite a few people milling around, which made it difficult for him to identify anything very distant. He was uneasy. He did not like the idea of being crept up upon without warning. He felt far too vulnerable.

People were moving in all directions as they shopped. It was very chaotic. There was an interesting mix of fashion, size, general appearance and demeanor amongst them. Suddenly Monika noticed James amidst the crowd a little further into the Mall. She leaned back towards Grai and Meyers, and without taking her eyes off her sighting, spoke so that both men could hear her above the din of the numerous nearby shoppers.

"There. Over there. It's James." she said it with certainty as she pointed in the direction of her sighting.

Meyers and Grai strained to see through the shoppers. They followed Monika's pointing finger and off in the distance, they saw two very determined men flanking each side of another man. The man in the center was being held by his arms as he was being forcefully escorted closer to them through the crowds. It was difficult to make out their faces through the crowd.

"Take it easy," Meyers cautioned Monika more

than Grai. "We don't want to spook them."

Grai strained to see more clearly the faces of the men delivering James. It was hard even for him with his greater height to get a good look through the crowd. He stood up as high as he could and tried to examine them.

As the men came closer Grai began to panic. He sensed something was wrong. Slowly they came more into view, and as they did, Grai realized that theses were not the faces of his associates. Instantly, he understood that this was a set up.

Without any warning, Grai drew out his gun from inside his jacket holster and grabbed hold of Monika, pulling her aside. As he did so he moved away from Meyers. The three approaching men noticed this sudden movement and quickened their pace. James and Monika's eyes met for an instant as she was being pulled away. There was fear and shock in her stare. Meyers caught the look of distress in the three approaching men's faces. There was a sense of urgency to their look. Meyers understood the look. He realized that something was wrong. He turned to check the object of their concern just as Grai was moving away with Monika.

"Wha…?! What…?!" Monika blurted out as she struggled against Grai. Grai put the gun barrel into her side. She felt the message it gave and stopped her fight. She dropped the briefcase as she was manhandled by Grai. Grai did not notice.

It did not take long for the commotion to be noticed by several shoppers in the immediate area. Grai's gun was drawn. Someone screamed and then someone else yelled:

"He's got a gun!"

"Shut up. Do as I say and no one will get hurt." Grai spoke loudly enough for all to hear.

The crowd began to panic. This made it easier for Grai to make his move away with Monika.

Meyers and the other men with James, who were all by now struggling to get through the panicking crowd and stop Grai, were slowed down by the desperate scramble of those in the Mall to get out of the way and to safety. The approaching men, as well as Meyers, had their own guns drawn but could not risk any injuries to those in the Mall. They would not be able to use their guns in such close quarters. Grai had anticipated this and taking advantage of the opportunity, he made his way with Monika under gun point to the glass door entrance. He opened the door, and continued his escape pulling Monika along with him back towards the sidewalk that they had earlier come along. He hurried down the walk with a resistant

Monika in tow.

Meyers, James and the other two men took up pursuit as soon as they could get through the crowd but Grai had a good head start. Once outside the building, Meyers stopped and aimed his gun at Grai who was within range but getting farther away. It was not a clear shot. He did not fire. The crowd was too close. This did not however, deter Grai, who noticing Meyers attempt, turned and fired at him, hitting him in the left upper leg. Meyers grabbed at his wounded leg. Blood covered his hand as he tried to block the bleeding from the bullet hole. He took several more steps, but the pain was overpowering. He tried to go on. Pain shot through him. He would not be able to pursue Grai. He cursed at his misfortune as his leg gave way and he fell to the ground.

James, who was just exiting the Mall, hurried to Meyers as Grai continued on to the parking lot and the car. Shooting Meyers had given Grai an even better lead.

"Are you okay?" James was kneeling down by Meyers and checking him.

"Yes. It's just my left leg. Get after him."

James squeezed Meyers right arm to comfort him.

"Give me your gun." Meyers complied and

James rose to continue the pursuit of Grai. The other men were still caught amongst the shoppers inside the Mall.

Along the path to the street they ran. The chase resembled one from the movies. In and around the crowded street they went. Grai was a fair distance ahead, but still in clear view. James pursued. He tried to pick up his pace to close the distance between them before Grai got completely away. The chase was on, but it made little difference. Grai was too far ahead. James could see Grai getting to his car at Fisherman's Wharf.

At the car, Grai opened the door and forced Monika in through the driver's side. James put more effort into his running after them. He had almost caught up as Grai was getting into the vehicle. But it was not close enough. James was about fifty feet away. Realizing that he was not going to get to them in time, James stopped and shouted to Grai,

"Stop it there Grai. There isn't any place you can go."

Grai smiled, "Don't be so sure."

"Let her go." James was threatening.

The people near the lot who now saw and heard what was going on, began to panic and instantly attempted to protect themselves by clearing out of the immediate area. Some dropped to the ground and others ran for cover wherever they thought they would be safe and out of the line of gun fire.

"Her? She's my insurance."

James aimed his gun at Grai and fired a shot, but missed. This action by James did not stop Grai from getting into the car and closing the door. James did not fire again. He had missed the moment. Grai was now in the car. James could not take the chance of Monika or an innocent bystander getting hurt by taking another shot. He lowered his gun and helplessly watched as Grai started the car and put it into reverse to pull away. James was at a loss as to what he could do next. As Grai prepared to back up, he noticed James' dilemma. He hadn't expected the gun shot, but when it had occurred and missed, he looked to James through the windshield and smirked.

During the split second that Grai's attention was more on James' shooting and less on her, Monika made a surprising move. Giving no warning, as Grai took his foot off the brake to put it on the accelerator, she slammed her left foot onto Grai's right foot and gas pedal. There was a squealing of the rear tires as they got a sudden burst of power. The car responded and backed up out of control at a high rate of speed.

Grai struggled against Monika to regain control of the situation, but Monika would not stop. She was determined. The car backed fiercely into the protective blocks at the edge of the parking lot. With a loud crash, it broke through the barrier and plunged out over into the air and then splashed trunk first into the cold water of the harbor. The car floated for a second and then, shifting to its front heavy end, sank like a stone into the dark ocean.

James was horrified by the sight. It had all happened so unpredictably fast. He rushed to the edge of the sea wall. As he powerlessly watched the car sinking the other two men from the Mall arrived and came to his side. James could see that Monika and Grai were still inside the car struggling as it sank below the surface. It was all happening so quickly. There was no time to think. They would not be able to get out before the vehicle was submerged. He had to do something.

Without regard for his own safety, James fit his gun securely behind his belt buckle and jumped feet first into the dark water as close to where the car sank as he could. The car could no longer be seen. Only the escaping bubbling air from within it was indicating its location. James swam over to the bubbling in the water. He took a deep breath and submerged himself into the water and swam down to the car.

The water was cold, deep and dark. There was very little natural light illuminating it. Monika and Grai had now stopped their fight with each other and were trying to escape from within the car, but the doors would not open and the power windows were fused shut. The water filled the interior rapidly. Monika and Grai tried to keep their noses and mouths up above its level to the very last bit of trapped air in the interior car roof. This air pocket was diminishing as the car continued to shift and sink. Finally, as the last little space of air escaped, Grai and Monika both took their last breath. There was not much time left for them and they each were acutely aware of the potential outcome if they could not get out soon. If they wanted to survive they had only a few more minutes. They redoubled their efforts at trying to get out of the car. They had to find a way out—now!

Both Monika and Grai began using their fists against the windows trying to break out of their watery tomb. It brought no result. They could not bring enough force through the water to break the glass. They were running out of breath and panicking. Monika let out a short scream with her last breath of air, but it was muzzled by the water. She passed out but her eyes remained glaringly open and fixed.

The car had settled onto the bottom as James reached it. His breath was not strong. He hurried to the passenger's side. It was very dark. The small amount of light filtering down through the surface allowed him, with difficulty, to see Monika. He was horrified as he viewed her lifeless gaze. Her breath had expired and her mouth was open. Though she was not yet dead, she held a vacant stare. James tried, by pounding on the window, to get her attention. She was not responsive. He panicked. He tried the door handle, but it did not work. He tried kicking through the window, but to no avail. Desperately he pulled out his gun and fired a few shots through the window. There was a muffled bang after each shot, followed by a high pitched hollow sound as the bullets pierced through the water. As the shots were fired, the floating James was pushed back by the force of their recoil and into a changed position within the water.

Small holes appeared in the glass. James swam closer to the car. He grabbed onto the door handle to secure himself and using the heal of his shoes, he struck several times at the holes in the window.

Now that the glass was weakened by the bullet holes, he was quickly able to smash through the window.

As soon as the window had shattered, James stretched inside the car, his breath almost gone. He grabbed onto and pulled Monika, who was now limp, out through the car window. There was not much time left to any of them. Grai was still in the car and like Monika, was motionless. He could not save them both. He made his decision and with Monika secured, James turned upward and swam with her the twenty feet to the surface. His breath was now gone. He pulled desperately through the water. The trip seemed to take an eternity, but finally he broke through into the surface. He let out a gasp for new air. In between gasps James turned and noted that the other two men from the Mall had arrived at the sea wall. He yelled to them,

"Grai's trapped in the car."

One of the men jumped into the water swam to the bubbling spot and dove down to the car and Grai.

James continued swimming with an unconscious Monika held under his left arm, to the sea wall. There was a large crowd gathered above looking over in shock. Meyers had now managed to arrive and was standing above. He shouted to James who was ten feet below in the water and almost at the sea wall,

"Hold on to the side. We'll get you out."

●

Early the next morning there was a large crowd gathered at Fisherman's Wharf as something was being pulled from the harbor. There was much noise as directions were being given to the work crews. Three scuba divers were in the water out of harm's way. Cables ran from out of the water and into a huge crane that suspended them. The order was given. The cables tightened and began to creak as they were being reeled in. The crane strained under an obviously heavy load. Within moments a large object broke through to the surface from its watery grave. It was a car. The vehicle was pulled completely clear of the water and allowed to hang. Liquid poured from the car as it was suspended above the water. It remained in that position for a few minutes. Then the crane began slowly to swing the car over to the dry dock; most of the water having been drained from it.

●

Monika awoke, it was mid morning. The sun was shining through the window behind her. As she wakened, she was becoming more and more disoriented. It was a strange room, not her own. She propped herself up on the bed so that she could better see where she was. She did not remember how she came to be here. The last thing she remembered was being in the car at Fisherman's Wharf and throwing her foot onto the accelerator. She recalled the car plunging through the barrier and into the water. She felt the impact and the rocking of the car as it changed direction and began to fill with the cold bay water, and rapidly sink.

She remembered struggling with Grai and then the darkness of being submerged beneath the water. She relived the moments in her mind. She felt the cold dark water upon her as the car filled. Both she and Grai had attempted to take whatever breaths of remaining air there were in the car. There had been just one last quickly stolen breath from inside the car near to the roof, before all of the trapped air in the car had escaped. She remembered her desperation as she knew that there was no escaping the car. She remembered her struggle to open the car door or break through the passenger window and then………nothing. Monika felt a cold shiver at these memories.

Now here she was in this place and…alive? She

considered for a moment that she might be dead and that this might be... She looked around the sparsely decorated room. It was painted with a high gloss off white paint. The ceiling was high and the walls were of a glossy institutional plaster. Around her bed upon the ceiling was a curtain track. A blue curtain was attached to the track and tied up out of the way against the wall. The floor was shiny, and the bed had a steel railing around it. She was alone... No. She was not dead. She now realized that she was in a hospital bed in a private room. She was safe. There was a nurse's call button on the wall close to her.

Lowering the rail, Monika leaned over to reach the button that was on the wall next to her bed and rang for the nurse. There was no indication that the button worked, so she pressed it several times and then lay back onto her bed. After a few moments there came a knock at the door, it opened and a blond man walked in.

"Hi. How are you?" William was smiling and carrying a bouquet of flowers. He was dressed in a suit. Monika was alarmed and not sure what to do. Not waiting for a verbal response, William walked over and handed the beautiful flowers to her, giving her a kiss as he did so. "I thought we'd lost you."

"Lost me? I don't get it. What are you doing here? Where are we?" Monika was astounded. Her head was pounding from the shock of William's presence.

"It's a very long story. You are in San Francisco Memorial."

"How did I get here?"

"I brought you."

"You?" she was not sure if she should believe him.

"Well, actually Meyers and me."

"You know Meyers?"

"Yes."

"And Grai?"

"Grai won't be bothering you again. We pulled him out of his car this morning."

"We? I don't understand. What is this all about? What happened to James?" Monika's tone gave away her disorientated state of mind.

"James is fine." William pulled a small wallet out of his jacket pocket and presented it to Monika in an attempt to calm her and prove his trustworthiness.

"CIA."

"What?"

"We are all part of the Company."

"All? Company?" This was too bizarre for her

to believe.

William tried to explain,

"We uncovered a security breach regarding your father's work and traced it to the FBI office in San Francisco. We went undercover as FBI agents, and soon came to realize that Grai was involved. Grai was trying to steal your father's work and sell it to the highest bidder, but we couldn't prove it. So we faked your parent's car crash. Nobody knew about it. I'm sorry you had to go through that, but it was the only way."

"And that day? The phone call, and your business meeting?" Monika's mind was confused and reaching out for some verification of the truth and whether or not she could trust what William was saying.

"Yes. It was all part of the plan. You had to believe that something was wrong and that your parents had mysteriously disappeared or…"

"I wouldn't have been convincing."

"Yes. It had to be that way. I couldn't come with you that day because I had to make the call and set things up."

"Oh." Monika felt betrayed.

"After you left to go to the store, I arrived. I had been waiting outside in a car down the street. I made a mess of the place and then took your parents into safe keeping."

"So they are alive?" she had a glimmer of hope.

"They were never in the car. I fed Grai false information to try and ferret him and any associates out into the open. We led him to believe that you had something in the briefcase. Something that would lead him to your father's notes. Grai never knew we were part of the Company. The risk to you was minimal. I'm sorry we couldn't let you know, but we had to find a way to expose him. We kept a close eye on you. James volunteered to help us to protect you. We put him in the school along with some others once we knew you would be working there. We weren't sure how or when Grai would act."

"Ms. Wembly?" Monika was checking.

"Yes." William smiled, understanding the reason behind Monika's question.

"She played her part well." Monika was sarcastic. "What about you and me?" she became bitter.

"I'm sorry. That wasn't meant to happen. I was meant to get to know you so I wouldn't be suspected being around all the time." William was apologetic.

"And James?

"He's one of us."

"So I guess that wasn't meant to be either? Just

a part of the plan. That's why he's not here?" Monika was hurt.

William did not respond.

Monika changed the direction of the conversation and demanded,

"What about my parents? Where are they?"

"It's a long story."

"I've got the time."

"I have someone here who can better explain it." William rose up and crossed over to open the door. Monika's parents entered,

"Mom. Dad." Monika was both elated and confused.

Her mother and father hurried over to the bed and hugged their daughter. There was so much they had to tell each other, but for the moment they were overtaken by their emotion of their reunion. It had been so long since they had been together. Tears filled their eyes and flowed down their faces as they hugged.

"Mom.......Dad....I...love......you." Monika was emotionally overwrought. It took all her strength to say these words before breaking down. Her parents comforted her.

After several moments of being consoled, they were distracted by a noise at the doorway. Monika looked up from her parent's embrace to the door.

A man came into view. Monika wiped the tears from her eyes in order to see better. Suddenly she knew who it was. She felt the presence of him.

"James?!" she called out questioningly and in shock.

Monika was overwhelmed. She was not sure what she should do, or who she could trust. So much had been thrust upon her in the last several minutes and she had not yet been able to sort out her conflicting emotions.

James made no verbal reply. He stood in the doorway. His eyes met her's giving a visual confirmation of his affection for her. Monika became comforted. She understood —he had come for her. He entered into the room.

Monika broke from her parents' embrace and rose from her bed. She ran to his open arms. They held each other tightly. She was so happy to be with him, and he with her. Monika suddenly pulled back from her embrace and looked into his eyes. "Was I just another part of your job?"

"No.—Maybe at first, but not now." He smiled and drew her closer. "I love you."

Monika welcomed his advance. He brought his lips to hers. Her heart raced. She was truly happy. She closed her eyes in anticipation and awaited his kiss.

Terence Munsey[*] lives in Richmond Hill, Ontario, Canada. He holds an M.A. from Stanford University in California, and writes mystery—intrigue as well as fantasy fiction. He is currently writing another book in his NATIONAL BESTSELLING series:

THE STONEMAN SERIES™

[*]Member of The Writer's Union of Canada

Order these other books by TERENCE MUNSEY:

The FLIGHT of the STONEMAN'S SON [1]

The KEEPER of THREE [1]

LABYRINTHS of LIGHT [1]

MARKS of STONE [2]

THEY of OLD [3]

OBSESSION [2]

EMERALD CITY [3]

Ask your bookstore to order
or
Mail Order

M U N S E Y   M U S I C

Box 511 Richmond Hill Ontario Canada L4C 4Y8

E-MAIL: terence_munsey@tvo.org
Visit our Web Site@
http://www.digiserve.com/stoneman/

Please add $2.00 shipping and handling costs for one book.
For each additional book per same order add $0.75 per book
to cover extra shipping costs.

[1] =$5.99 Canada ($4.99 U.S.)
[2] =$6.99 Canada ($5.99 U.S.)
[3] =$7.99 Canada ($6.99 U.S.)

Though we try to maintain prices, prices are subject to change
without notice. Mail orders allow 2 to 3 weeks delivery.